Road Maps

for the

Non-Pauline Epistles

and

Revelation

Contents

Preface

A.G. Clarke's *Analytical Studies in the Psalms*, Graham Scroggie's *Bible Handbook* and *Guide to the Gospel's*, Griffith Thomas' works, as well as those of John Phillips, John G. Butler, Warren Wiersbe, Harold Willmington (just to name a few) have inspired countless Bible students, pastors and teachers to explain the text of Scripture in a systematic, orderly exposition, using outlines to communicate God's glorious truth to others.

In 2006, George Zemek wrote a book called, *Road Maps for the Psalms: Inductive Preaching Outlines Based on the Hebrew Text*. It too has been a help to Bible expositors all over the world. While the title of this volume is obviously barrowed from Dr. Zemek's, it makes no claim to be as exegetically precise or based upon detailed diagrammatical analysis.

This book is intended as an initial roadmap for other adventurers to explore the infinitely beautiful terrain of this portion of God's Word. Not every geographical marker has been mapped—nor could it be. But it is a start to help you navigate through the major highways and back trails of the non-Pauline epistles and Revelation.

The varied formats of the different authors of this volume have been, for the most part, kept in an attempt to highlight each author's own style and emphasis. It is our prayer that the different styles and approaches to outlining are not a distraction, but rather an encouragement to see how others with a high view of the text have seen it, and help you then make your own roadmap, which accurately reflects the hallowed territory, yet is unique to your own journey and ministry context.

You will also find Dr. James Price's website of great help (www.jamesdprice.com), as well as James Bartsch's (www.wordexplain.com). Both of these men have crafted excellent expository and exegetical outlines of most of the books of the Bible.

May God bless you as you seek to know His Son through His Word—and then make Him known.

Kress Biblical Resources 2016

HEBREWS

Kress Biblical Resources

Overview Outline of Hebrews

Jesus, the Son of God, is the final and full expression of God's Redemptive Program—therefore hold fast your confession and draw near to God through Him, rather than return to the Old Covenant expressions of God's redemptive plan. [*]

Part One—Jesus, the Son of God, is the Better Message, Messenger, and Minister of God's Salvation (1:1-4:13)

I. He is superior to the prophets, the angels, and the OT Law they delivered from God—therefore we must hold dear the revelation and salvation that is in Christ (1:1-2:18)

A. Jesus is greater than the prophets and their message—He is the final and full revelation of God (1:1-4)

B. Jesus is greater than the angels and the Law they escorted—He is God come in the flesh (1:5-2:18)

II. He is superior to Moses—therefore we must hold fast our confession and find our rest in Christ (3:1-4:13)

A. The exhortation to consider Jesus' superiority to Moses—He is not simply a faithful servant in God's house, He is a faithful Son over God's house (3:1-6)

B. The expository application to guard against unbelief, hold fast to our confidence in Christ, and find our rest in Him (3:7-4:13)

Part Two—Jesus, the Son of God, is the Better High Priest and Mediator of a Better Covenant [He is a Better Mediator with a Better Ministry] (4:14-10:18)

I. He is the superior High Priest—therefore we must hold fast our confession and draw near to the throne of grace (4:14-7:28)

A. Jesus has a more exalted position—therefore hold fast and draw near (4:14-16)

B. Jesus has a more excellent priesthood—part one (5:1-10)

---

[*] **Hold fast** our confession and **draw near** to God—repeated exhortation (4:14, 16; 10:22, 23; cf. 3:1, 6, 14; 6:18; 7:25; 10:1; 11:6; 12:18, 22)

C. WARNING #3: Jesus has a more exclusive priority, which has eternal implications—therefore exercise faith and patience, in hope until the end (5:11-6:20)

D. Jesus has a more excellent priesthood—part two (7:1-28)

II. He is the Mediator of the superior covenant—therefore we must hold fast our hope and endure in the faith (8:1-10:39)

A. The New Covenant has better promises (8:1-13)

B. The New Covenant is effected in a better sanctuary with a better sacrifice—part one (9:1-14)

C. The New Covenant is effected in a better sanctuary with a better sacrifice—part two (9:15-10:18)

[D. WARNING #4: The New Covenant access we have compels us to hold fast to Christ and to endure in the faith (10:19-39)*]

Part Three—New Covenant Faith in Jesus, the Son of God, is the Only Acceptable Way to Worship God (10:19-13:25)

I. Let us draw near, hold fast, and encourage one another in the sufficiency of Christ (10:19-25)

A. Let us draw near to God in worship (10:19-22)

B. Let us hold fast the confession of our hope (10:23)

C. Let us encourage one another to love and good deeds (10:24-25)

II. WARNING #4: Let us consider the consequences of rejecting Christ and the New Covenant (10:26-39)

A. If you reject New Covenant access through Christ, there no longer remains a sacrifice for sins (10:26-27)

B. If you reject New Covenant access through Christ, the punishment is infinitely more severe than disregarding the Old Covenant Law of Moses (v. 28-31)

C. If you respond in faith and do not shrink back, there is great reward (10:32-39)

---

* alternate outline depending on the division of the text. These points are perhaps better under the next section.

III. Let us remember those who endured in living by the faith (11:1-12:3)

A. The summary statement concerning living by faith (11:1-2)

B. The survey of living by faith in the Old Testament (11:3-38)

C. The summary statement concerning living faith *in the Old Testament era* (11:39-40)

D. The specific application concerning living by faith in the New Testament era (12:1-3)

IV. WARNING #5: Let us endure in our faith and embrace the discipline of the Lord—and let no one come short of the grace of God and refuse the Word of God (12:4-29)

A. Embrace the discipline of the Lord (12:4-11)

B. Exercise your faith by pursuing holiness rather than temporary relief (12:12-17)

C. Express your gratitude for the privilege of New Covenant worship by staying faithful to New Covenant worship (12:18-29)

V. Let us worship God by a life of faith (13:1-25)

A. The life of faith and the practice of love (13:1-6)

B. The life of faith and the practice of Old Covenant worship (13:7-16)

C. The life of faith and the practice of fellowship (13:17-25)

Introductory Matters

I. The author

A. The human author

1. He is unnamed

2. He wrote to those who knew him, and accepted his authority (13:17-19, 22-25 [note v. 24, he was either writing to Italy or from Italy, cf. Acts 18:2])

3. He was an expert in the Old Testament Scriptures, and their relationship to Christ's Person and work

4. He was not one of the Twelve (2:3-4)

B. The divine author (2 Tim. 3:16-17)

II. The audience

A. The original audience

1. Professing believers in Christ, facing persecution (1:1-2; 2:1-4; 3:1, 12; 4:2; 13:22)—but they were immature and some perhaps in danger of apostasy (5:11-:6:9; 10:26-39; 12:3-4)

2. Professing believers who were most likely Jewish or Jewish proselytes. They were quite familiar with the Old Testament and particularly concerned with the priestly functions (1:3; 2:17; 3:1; 4:14-15; 5:1-6; 6:19-20; 7:11-12, 23-28; 8:1-6; 9:6-8, 11-14, 23-28; 10:1-4, 11-14, 19-23; 12:24, 28; 13:9-16)

B. The current audience [21st century professing believers]

III. The aim

A. **Exaltation** of Christ's Person and work—to emphatically show that Jesus, the Son of God, is the final and full expression of God's redemptive program [He is superior to all Old Testament expressions of God's plan, because the Son is the greater Person, Prophet, Priest, Propitiaion, and Provider of God's Salvation]

1. He is the better Word from God (1:1-4)

2. He is the better guardian of God's Word than angels—since He is God come in the flesh (1:6, 8, 10-12; 2:1-4, 14-15)

3. He is the better minister over God's people than Moses—Moses was a servant of God, but Jesus is the Son of God, who has authority over God's work (3:2-6)

4.   He is the better minister of God's rest than Joshua—He is our Sabbath rest (4:8-10)

5.   He is the better High Priest (5:1-7:28)

6.   He is the Priest of the better covenant (8:1-6)

7.   He ratified that covenant in the better sanctuary—heaven (9:11)

8.   He ratified that covenant with a better sacrifice (9:12-14, 23-24)

9.   Faith in Christ is the better, and now only way to draw near to God (10:14, 18, 19-23; 11:1, 6; 13:12-15)

B.   Endurance of believers in their confession of faith—to emphatically warn and exhort professing Jewish believers to go on to maturity in their faith, holding fast their confession and drawing near to God through Christ rather than turning back in faithlessness to the Old Covenant expressions of worship which are passing away **(13:22; cf. 2:1-4; 3:7-9; 4:1-13; 5:11-6:9; 10:26-31; 12:14-17, 25** [for "hold fast" and "draw near," see 4:14, 16; 10:22, 23; cf. 3:1, 6, 14; 6:18; 7:25; 10:1; 11:6; 12:18, 22]**)**

C.   Encouragement of those persecuted for their faith in Christ—to comfort believers in their persecutions **(11:1-12:13; 13:12-14 [cf. 10:32-34; 12:4])**

D.   Edification of those faced with false teaching—to alert believers of doctrinal and practical error **(13:7-10, 17)**

E.   Entreaty—to ask for prayer, to foster fellowship, and to express future plans **(13:18-19, 23-24)**

Detailed Outline of Hebrews

Jesus, the Son of God, is the final and full expression of God's redemptive program—therefore hold fast your confession and draw near to God through Him, rather than returning to the Old Covenant expressions of God's redemptive plan. [*]

Part One—Jesus, the Son of God, is the Better Message, Messenger, and Minister of God's Salvation (1:1-4:13)

I. He is superior to the prophets, the angels, and the OT Law they delivered from God—therefore we must hold dear the revelation and salvation that is in Christ (1:1-2:18)

A. Jesus is greater than the prophets and their message—He is the final and full revelation of God (1:1-4)

1. The revelation of God in the Old Testament is glorious and gracious—but necessarily incomplete (1:1)

    a. *The incalculable grace of God's Word in the prophets (1:1a)*

    b. *The incomplete nature of God's Word in the prophets (1:1b)*

2. The revelation of God in the Son is full and final—even more glorious and gracious, because the Son is by nature God (1:2-4)

    a. *The Son is the Word of God to us in these last days (1:2a)*

    b. *The Son is the Possessor of all things (1:2b)*

    c. *The Son is the Creator and Controller of history (1:2c)*

    d. *The Son is the Revealer [visible manifestation] of God Himself (1:3a)*

    e. *The Son is the Sustainer of all things (1:3b)*

    f. *The Son is the Redeemer from sins (1:3c)*

    g. *The Son is the exalted Ruler whose work of redemption is finished (1:3d)*

    h. *The Son is the greater messenger—since He possesses a name that is more excellent than the angels (1:4)*

---

[*] **Hold fast** our confession and **draw near** to God—repeated exhortation (4:14, 16; 10:22, 23; cf. 3:1, 6, 14; 6:18; 7:25; 10:1; 11:6; 12:18, 22)

B. Jesus is greater than the angels and the Law they escorted—He is God come in the flesh (1:5-2:18)

1. The exegetical proof that the Son is greater than the angels because of His deity and position as Messiah (1:5-14)

   a. *He is the promised messianic Son—no angel ever received such a designation (v. 5; cf. Ps. 2:7; 2 Sam. 7:14; 1 Chron. 17:13)*

      i. Psalm. 2:7—The pledge to Messiah

      ii. 2 Samuel 7:14/1 Chron. 17:13—The promise to David

   b. *He is to be worshipped by the angels of God (v. 6; cf. Ps. 97:7; Deut. 32:43 LXX)*

      i. The context of His coming (v. 6a)

      ii. Psalm 97:7/Deuteronomy 32:43 LXX—The command to the angels (v. 6b)

   c. *He is honored by God as God—angels are servants (v. 7-9; cf. Ps. 45:6-7; 104:4)*

      i. Psalm 104:4—God's description of the ministry of angels (v. 7)

      ii. Psalm 45:6-7—God's declaration of the majesty of the Son (v. 8-9)

   d. *He is the eternal Creator—the unchanging, everlasting Lord over history (v. 10-12; cf. Ps. 102:25-27)*

      i. Psalm 102:25—The Son is the omnipotent Creator (v. 10)

      ii. Psalm 102:26-27—The Son is the unchanging, everlasting Lord (v. 11-12)

   e. *He is the exalted Ruler awaiting His kingdom—angels are servants (v. 13-14; cf. Ps. 110:1)*

      i. Psalm 110:1—The Son is the exalted Sovereign awaiting His kingdom (v. 13)

      ii. The angels are ministering spirits, sent out for the service of believers (v. 14)

2. The expository application to pay close attention to the gospel of salvation in the Son, and be careful not to drift from it [WARNING #1] (2:1-4)

    a. *The charge—pay much closer attention to God's Word in His Son (v. 1)*

    b. *The caution—consider the consequences of a lack of concern (v. 2-4)*

        i.   Consider the just consequences of disobeying the Old Testament Law (v. 2)

        ii. Consider the greater consequences of disregarding New Testament salvation in the Son (v. 3a)

        iii. Consider the Person and divine power that confirmed the message of salvation in the New Testament (3b-4)

             aa. The Lord Himself was the Messenger (and the Message) of salvation (v. 3b)

             bb. The Apostles/eyewitnesses confirmed the message of salvation in Him (v. 3c)

             cc. God confirmed their testimony through miraculous signs and gifts of the Holy Spirit (v. 4)

3. The exegetical proof that the Son is greater than the angels because of His humanity and position as High Priest (2:5-18)

    a. *God's plan for creation is that it be subject to man, not angels—Jesus' incarnation, redemption and exaltation inaugurate this (v. 5-9; cf. Psalm 8:4-6)*

        i.   God's plan did not subject the world to come to angels (v. 5)

        ii. God's plan is for man to rule all things (v. 6-8ab; cf. Ps. 8:4-6)

             aa. The citation introduced—a testimony of God's exalted plan for man (v. 6a)

             bb. The citation quoted—Psalm 8:4-6 (v. 6b-8a)

             cc. The commentary made (v. 8b)

        iii. God's plan is not yet fully manifest (v. 8c)

  iv. God's plan is inaugurated in Jesus (v. 9)

    aa. The incarnation (v. 9a)

    bb. The passion (v. 9b)

    cc. The exaltation (v. 9c)

    dd. The redemption (v. 9d)

 b. *God's plan for bringing <u>many</u> sons to glory necessitated Jesus' incarnation, suffering, and death—so that He could be a faithful and merciful High Priest (v. 10-18)*

  i. Jesus, through suffering, became the Pioneer of our salvation (v. 10)

  ii. Jesus, through the incarnation, became our Brother (v. 11-13; cf. Ps. 22:22; Is. 8:17-18)

    aa. The assertion (v. 11)

    bb. The quotations (v. 12-13; cf. Psalm 22:22; Is. 8:17-18)

  iii. Jesus, through His death, became our Deliverer from death and the devil (v. 14-15)

    aa. The reason for the incarnation (v. 14a)

    bb. The result of His life, death, and resurrection (v. 14b-15)

     The defeat of the devil, who held the power of death

     The emancipation of men from the fear of death

  iv. Jesus, through His suffering, became our merciful and faithful High Priest (v. 16-18)

    aa. He came to take hold of the seed of Abraham—not angels (v. 16)

    bb. He came to be a merciful and faithful high priest (v. 17ab)

    cc. He came to make the satisfactory atonement for sins (v. 17c)

    dd. He came to answer the cry of those who are tempted (v. 18)

II. He is superior to Moses—therefore we must hold fast our confession and find our rest in Christ (3:1-4:13)

A. The exhortation to consider Jesus' superiority to Moses—He is not simply a faithful servant in God's house, He is a faithful Son over God's house (3:1-6)

1. The call to consider Jesus (3:1-2)

   a. *Because of what He has done for us (v. 1a)*

   b. *Because it is commanded (v. 1b)*

   c. *Because of who He is (v. 1c-2)*

      i. Jesus is the One sent from God (v. 1c)

      ii. Jesus is the High Priest of our confession (v. 1d)

      iii. Jesus is faithful to God, even as Moses was (v. 2)

2. The comparison between Jesus and Moses (3:3-6a)

   b. *The comparison between the Creator and the created—Jesus is God, Moses is not (v. 3-4)*

      i. The illustration of the builder and the house (v. 3)

      ii. The explanation and implication—Jesus is God (v. 4)

   c. *The comparison between a Son and a servant—Jesus is the Son, Moses is a servant (v. 5-6a)*

      i. Moses was a faithful servant in God's house (v. 5)

      ii. Christ is a faithful Son over God's house (v. 6a)

3. The concern we must have in light of Jesus' surpassing glory (v. 6b)

B. The expository application to guard against unbelief, hold fast to our confidence in Christ, and find our rest in Him [WARNING #2] (3:7-4:13)

1. The exposition of Psalm 95:7-11 (3:7-19)

   a. *The biblical quotation—Psalm 95:7-11 (v. 7-11)*

      i. The context of Psalm 95:7-11 (v. 7a)

      ii. The call of Psalm 95:7-8 (v. 7b-8)

      iii. The critical issue of unbelief in Psalm 95:9 (v. 9)

      iv. The consequences of unbelief in Psalm 95:10-11 (v. 10-11)

   b. *The personal application—an exhortation to keep the faith (v. 12-14)*

      i. Examine your faith (v. 12)

      ii. Encourage one another day after day (v. 13)

      iii. Endure in your initial confidence in Christ (v. 14)

   c. *The further explanation—the Psalm depicts God's pronouncement on an unbelieving generation (v. 15-19)*

      i. The repetition of Psalm 95:7b-8 as a reminder of the passage under discussion (v. 15)

      ii. The exposition of Psalm 95:7-11 via questions and answer (v. 16-19)

         aa. The first question and answer—who provoked God when they had heard? [Those who followed Moses out of Egypt] (v. 16)

         bb. The second question and answer—with whom was God angry with for forty years? [Those who sinned] (v. 17)

         cc. The third question and answer—to whom did God swear they would not enter His rest? [Those who were disobedient] (v. 18)

      iii. The interpretation of Psalm 95:7-11 as to the problem of that generation (v. 19)

2. The emphasis in Psalm 95 on entering the promised rest (4:1-13)

   a. *The exhortation—to be sure to enter God's rest by faith (v. 1-2)*

      i. We should shake with fear at the thought of falling short of God's promised rest (v. 1)

      ii. We should see to it that our hearing of God's Word is met with genuine trust (v. 2)

   b. *The explanation—in God's sovereignty, the promised rest is still available for those who believe (v. 3-10)*

      i. We who have believed are entering God's rest (v. 3a)

      ii. We must see "Today" as the day to believe and enter God's rest (v. 3b-10)

         aa. God's rest can be divinely denied, though it has been available since the foundation of the world (v. 3b-5)

            God's rest was divinely denied to those who provoked His wrath (v. 3b)

            God's rest has been available from the foundation of the world (v. 3c-4)

            God's rest was divinely denied to that unbelieving generation (v. 5)

         bb. God's rest is still available "Today" for the people of God (v. 6-10)

            There remains an entrance into His rest (v. 6a)

            There is the example of those who failed to enter it because of disobedient unbelief (v. 6b)

            There is a sovereignly appointed "Today" to enter into it by faith (v. 7)

            The promised rest was not fulfilled in Joshua's day (v. 8)

            There remains a Sabbath rest for the people of God (v. 9-10) *c.*   *The exhortation repeated—be diligent to enter God's rest (v. 11-13)*

          i.   We must make every effort to enter God's rest—so that no one will fall like those who followed Moses in the wilderness, but were really disobedient [We must make sure we trust God's Son] (v. 11)

          ii. We must make sure we do not disregard God's Word[*] (v. 12)

               aa. It is living

               bb. It is effective

               cc. It is sharp

               dd. It is piercing

               ee. It is discerning

          iii. We must make sure we do not disregard God's day of reckoning (v. 13)

               aa. He sees everything

               bb. He sees everything perfectly

               cc. We will give an account to Him

Part Two—Jesus, the Son of God, is the Better High Priest and Mediator of a Better Covenant [He is a Better Mediator with a Better Ministry] (4:14-10:18)

I. He is the superior High Priest—therefore we must hold fast our confession and draw near to the throne of grace (4:14-7:28)

A. Jesus has a more exalted position—therefore hold fast and draw near (4:14-16)

    1. Encouragement #1: The exalted position of the Son as heavenly High Priest gives us hope to hold fast (4:14a)

       a.   *The implicit need for encouragement (cf. 4:11-13)*

       b.   *The exalted position He has as High Priest*

       c.   *The exalted place in which He ministers*

---

[*] The thesis statement of verse 12 is adapted from R. Kent Hughes, *Hebrews* Vol. 1, p. 119.

       d.   The exalted name He possesses

2.   Exhortation #1: Hold fast your confession of faith in Christ (4:14b)

3.   Encouragement #2: The express sympathy of the Son gives us hope to draw near (4:15)

       a.   He understands what it is like to be subject to human frailty

       b.   He has been tempted in all things as we are

       c.   He is holy—thus His ministry is perfect

4.   Exhortation #2: Draw near to the throne of grace for help (4:16)

       a.   The privilege and responsibility we have in this difficult life (v. 16a)

       b.   The purpose and results we can expect (v. 16b)

B. Jesus has a more excellent priesthood—part one (5:1-10)

1.   The characteristics of the Aaronic high priest's ministry (5:1-4)

       a. His humanity—The high priest was a man appointed on behalf of men in the worship of God (v. 1)

       b. His sympathy—The high priest was subject to weakness and ministers in compassion (v. 2)

       c. His ministry—The high priest offered sacrifices for sins (v. 3)

       d. His authority—The high priest was chosen by God for this ministry (v. 4)

2.   The corresponding character of Christ's Melchizedekian high priestly ministry (5:5-10)

       a. His authority—Christ was chosen by God to be high priest (v. 5-6)

          i.   He was honored by God, being designated Messianic Son (v. 5; cf. Psalm 2:7)

          ii.   He was honored by God, being designated as Melchizedekian Priest (v. 6; cf. Ps. 110:4)

       b. His humanity—Christ was a man appointed on behalf of men in the worship of God (v. 7)

    c.   *His sympathy—Christ was subject to weakness and ministers in compassion (v. 7b-8)*

    d.   *His ministry—Christ offered the perfect sacrifice for sins and is the source of eternal salvation (v. 9-10)*

       i.   His perfect offering—eternal salvation (v. 9)

       ii.   His priesthood—according to the order of Melchizedek (v. 10)

C. WARNING #3: Jesus has a more exclusive priority, which has eternal implications—therefore exercise faith and patience, in hope until the end (5:11-6:20)

    1. The confrontation of spiritual immaturity (5:11-14)

       a.   *The details of the Melchizedekian priesthood are not easy for the spiritually lazy (v. 11)*

       b.   *The diminished capacity to understand is because of a very limited spiritual diet (v. 12-14)*

          i.   By this time you ought to be teachers, but you are in need of elementary instruction (v. 12)

          ii.   Becoming mature involves experience in the word and training in discernment (v. 13-14)

             aa.   The immature are inexperienced in the word of righteousness (v. 13)

             bb.   The mature are active in analyzing/discerning good from bad [doctrine] (v. 14)

    2. The call to press on to maturity (6:1-3)

       a.   *The elementary teaching about the Christ (v. 1-2)*

          i.   Going beyond the elementary and foundational (v. 1a)

          ii.   Such as repentance from dead works and faith toward God (v. 1bc)

          iii.   Such as teaching about washings and laying on of hands (v. 2a)

          iv.   Such as teaching about the resurrection of the dead and eternal judgment (v. 2c)

       b.   *The exhortation and intent to press on to maturity (v. 1, 3)*

          i.   The exhortation to advance spiritually (v. 1)

      ii.   The intent to do so—with God's sovereign enabling (v. 3)

3.   The case of those who fall away (6:4-8)

      a.   *The impossibility of renewal again to repentance (v. 4, 6)*

      b.   *The implications of the grammar and the imagery of the language (v. 4-6)*

          i.   Note the impersonal grammar rather than direct address (v. 4-6)

          ii.   Note the imagery that depicts either those who have been actually born again, or those thoroughly instructed in and associated with the gospel (v. 4-5)

          iii. Note the interpretive difficulty of "having fallen away" (v. 6a)

          iv. Note the issue at stake when one has "fallen away" (v. 6b)

      c.   *The illustration from farming (v. 7-8)*

          i.   Ground that brings forth fruit receives a blessing from God (v. 7)

          ii.   Ground that brings forth thorns and thistles ends up being burned (v. 8)

      d.   *The interpretations suggested*

          i.   Genuine believer who falls away—loss of eternal salvation
              aa. Can never be saved again

              bb. Contradicts numerous other passages of Scripture (cf. John 6:37, 39, 40, 44; 10:27-30; Rom. 8:29-39; Eph. 1:13-14; 4:30; Phil. 1:6; 1 Pet. 1:5; 5:10; 2 Pet. 2:4-9)

          ii.   Hypothetical situation to illustrate the foolishness of considering turning back to Judaism

              aa. Does fit with the phrase in 6:9, "though we are speaking in this way"

              bb. Difficulty in explaining how a hypothetical scenario that can't actually happen serves to warn the audience

          iii. Genuine believer who falls away—temporal judgment and loss of eternal reward

              aa. Does have some support from other Scriptures

              bb. Difficulty in explaining 6:9

        iv.   Professed believer who falls away—loss of ability to repent, no more opportunity for salvation

            aa.   Does perhaps account for those like Judas

            bb.   Difficulty with the terminology of v. 4-6

    e.   *The intent of the paragraph that must not be missed—this is a grave warning to press on to maturity and persevere in the faith, or face horrifying consequences (v. 6b, 7-8)*

        i.   Consider that repentance is impossible for those who fall away (v. 6a)

        ii.   Consider the reproach falling away would bring on Christ (v. 6b)

        iii.   Consider the results of fruitfulness [Divine blessing] (v. 7)

        iv.   Consider the results of fruitlessness [Severe discipline or possibly even eternal judgment] (v. 8)

4.   The call and comfort to continue in the faith (6:9-12)

    a.   *The encouragement concerning the evidences of salvation (v. 9-10)*

        i.   The comforting address (v. 9a)

        ii.   The conviction of the author (v. 9b)

        iii.   The character of God in regard to the concrete evidences of faith (v. 10)

    b.   *The exhortation to earnestly continue in the faith till the end (v. 11-12)*

        i.   Earnestly continue in the faith until the end (v. 11)

        ii.   Evidence trust and longsuffering like those who inherit the promises (v. 12)

5.   The call and comfort to hold on to our heavenly hope (6:13-20)

    a.   *The character and promise of God in regard to Abraham's hope (v. 13-15)*

        i.   The confirming oath to Abraham explained (v. 13)

        ii.   The context of God's oath to Abraham is vital (v. 14; cf. Gen. 22:17)

       iii.   The confirmation of the promise came after testing (v. 15)

   b.   *The character and promise of God in regard to our hope [Christ's high priestly ministry according to the order of Melchizedek] (v. 16-20)*

       i.   The confirming oath further explained as an indisputable guarantee (v. 16)

       ii.   The confirming oath in relation to New Testament believers—The indisputable guarantee of our hope in Christ (v. 17)

       ii.   The character of God in regard to His promise—The impossibility of God lying as yet another guarantee concerning Christ's priesthood on our behalf (v. 18a)

       iii.   The comfort and call to seize the hope set before us—The intercessory ministry of Christ brings us directly into God's presence (v. 18b-20)

          aa.   The characterization of those who believe (v. 18b)

          bb.   The comfort and call to seize the hope set before us (v. 18c)

          cc.   The character of that hope (v. 19)

          cc.   The Caretaker/Guarantor of our hope (v. 20)

D. Jesus has a more excellent priesthood—part two (7:1-28)

   1.   The superiority of Melchizedek to Levi established (7:1-10)

     a.   *The Genesis reference to Melchizedek summarized and explained (v. 1-3)*

       i.   The summary of the biblical reference (v. 1-2a; cf. Gen. 14:18-20)

       ii.   The significance of Melchizedek's name and position (v. 2b)

       iii.   The similarity Melchizedek has to the Son of God (v. 3) *b.*   *The greatness of Melchizedek stated and established (v. 4-10)*

        i.   His pre-eminence over Abraham (v. 4-7)

            aa.   Abraham gave him a tenth of the choicest spoils (v. 4)

            bb.   Abraham's descendants, the Levitical priests collect a tenth from the people (v. 5)

            cc.   Abraham gave a tenth and received a blessing from a non-Levitical priest—and without a doubt the lesser is blessed by the greater (v. 6-7)

        ii.   His pre-eminence over Levi (and thus the Levitical priests) (v. 8-10)

            aa.   The Levitical priesthood is temporary, but the Melchizedekian is permanent (v. 8)

            bb.   The Levitical priests paid tithes to Melchizedek by virtue of their identification with Abraham (v. 9-10)

2.   **The superiority of the Melchizedekian priesthood to the Aaronic priesthood examined (7:11-19)**

    a.   *Perfection could not be attained through the Levitical priesthood and the Law associated with it (v. 11)*

    b.   *Perfection comes only through a change in priesthood and Law (v. 12-19)*

        i.   The Levitical priesthood and the Levitical Law are inextricably bound (v. 12)

        ii.   The Lord's priesthood is not as a descendant of Levi (v. 13-14)

        iii.   The limitless life of the Priest spoken of in Psalm 110:4 insures perfection and a better hope, through which we draw near to God (15-19)

            aa.   The new order of worship is based on the power of an indestructible life (v. 15-16)

            bb.   The new order of worship is based on a permanent priesthood (v. 17)

            cc.   The new order of worship through Christ offers a better hope and intimacy with God—in contrast to the Levitical Law, which was weak and could never actually make the worshipper holy (v. 18-19)

3. The superiority of Jesus' priestly ministry explained (7:20-28)

    a. *He is appointed by divine oath [not genealogical succession] (v. 20-21)*

        i.   The surety of the divine oath (v. 20-21a)

        ii. The Scripture that records it (v. 21b)

    b. *He has become the guarantee of a better covenant (v. 22)*

    c. *He holds His priesthood permanently (v. 23-24)*

        i.   The Levitical priesthood required many priests because of death (v. 23)

        ii. The Lord's priesthood continues forever (v. 24)

    d. *He is able to save forever those who draw near to God through Him (v. 25)*

    e. *He is holy and exalted above the heavens (v. 26)*

    f. *He offered up one, all-sufficient sacrifice (v. 27)*

    g. *He is the perfect High Priest appointed directly by God (v. 28)*

II. He is the Mediator of the superior covenant—therefore we must hold fast our hope and endure in the faith (8:1-10:39)

A. The New Covenant has better promises (8:1-13)

1. The summary of Christ's superior priesthood (8:1-6)

    a. *He sits exalted at the right hand of God (v. 1)*

    b. *He serves in a superior tabernacle (v. 2)*

    c. *He offered a superior sacrifice (v. 3)*

    d. *He is the priest of a superior covenant (v. 4-6)*

        i.   He is not an Old Covenant priest (v. 4)

        ii. He does not serve under the Old Covenant—which is merely an earthly copy that foreshadows heavenly worship (v. 5)

        iii. He is the Mediator of a better covenant (v. 6)

2.   The superiority of the New Covenant promises (8:7-13)

     a.   *The problem with the Old Covenant (v. 7-9)*

         i.   The premise stated (v. 7)

         ii.   The problem was the disobedience of those bound by the Old Covenant [It was a conditional covenant, based on man's obedience] (v. 8a)

         iii.   The promise of the New Covenant came because Israel did not abide by the Old Covenant (v. 8b-9)

     b.   *The promises of the New Covenant (v. 10-12)*

         i.   The New Covenant would come "after those days" [after Israel's rejection of her King] (v. 10a)

         ii.   The New Covenant is internal, and intimate in divine rule—rather than an external law and national theocracy (v. 10b)

         iii.   The New Covenant is personally efficacious, with guaranteed regeneration—rather than dependent upon societal exhortation (v. 11)

         iv.   The New Covenant can never be broken because it promises mercy and forgiveness of sins—rather than being contingent on national obedience [Note the unconditional, unilateral nature of the New Covenant—everyone who is in covenant will know the Lord and receive mercy and forgiveness] (v. 12)

     c.   *The pre-eminence of the New Covenant (v. 13)*

         i.   In giving the New, God has made the first obsolete (v. 13a)

         ii.   Whatever is obsolete is ready to vanish (v. 13b)

B.   The New Covenant is effected in better sanctuary with a better sacrifice—part one (9:1-14)

1.   The earthly sanctuary and symbolism of Old Covenant worship (v. 1-10)

     a.   *The sanctuary and service of the first covenant introduced (v. 1)*

     b.   *The sanctuary of the first covenant described (v. 2-5)*

         i.   The holy place (v. 2)

         ii.   The Holy of Holies (v. 3-5)

    c.   *The service of the first covenant described (v. 6-10)*

        i.   The service in the holy place [was] continual (v. 6)

        ii.   The service in the Holy of Holies [was] singular—once a year (v. 7)

        iii.   The significance—direct access to God [was] not available under the old system of worship (v. 8-9a)

        iv.   The sacrifices of the Old Covenant also could not make the worshiper perfect in conscience (v. 9b-10)

2.   The exalted sanctuary and superiority of New Covenant worship (v. 11-14)

    a.   *The sanctuary of the New Covenant in which Christ ministers as high priest (v. 11)*

    b.   *The superiority of Christ's sacrifice, service, and sanctification of those who worship through Him (v. 12-14)*

        i.   The superiority of Christ's sacrifice and ministry of redemption (v. 12)

        ii.   The superiority of Christ's cleansing in regard to the worshipper (v. 13-14)

C. The New Covenant is effected in a better sanctuary with a better sacrifice—part two (9:15-10:18)

1.   The necessity of a sacrificial death in the ratification of a covenant (9:15-22)

    a.   *The reason for Christ's sacrifice—to mediate the New Covenant, redeem sinners, and secure an eternal inheritance for His people (v. 15)*

    b.   *The requirement of death in regard to a covenant (v. 16-17)*

    c.   *The requirement of death in regard to the first covenant (v. 18-21)*

        i.   Even the first covenant came through blood (v. 18)

        ii.   Exodus 24:3-8; Num. 7:1 (v. 19-21)

    d.   *The requirement of death in regard to the forgiveness of sins (v. 22; cf. Lev. 17:11)*

2.   The necessity of a superior sacrifice to sanctify heavenly worship and to save those who trust in Christ (9:23-28)

a.   *Christ's sacrifice is superior because it sanctifies His ministry in heaven itself (v. 23-24)*

b.   *Christ's sacrifice is superior because it sufficiently deals with sin, once for all (v. 25-26)*

c.   *Christ's sacrifice is superior because it secures salvation for those who eagerly await Him (v. 27-28)*

3.   The necessity of a submissive Savior and His selfless offering of Himself, once for all (10:1-10)

a.   *The inadequacy of the Old Covenant sacrifices to perfect the worshiper and take away sin (v. 1-4)*

i.   The assertion: The Law and its sacrifices cannot make the worshiper complete before God (v. 1)

ii.   The argument: (v. 2-3)

aa.   If OT sacrifices could make the worshiper complete before God, they would have ceased to be offered, having cleansed the worshiper completely (v. 2)

bb.   But in those sacrifices there is a reminder of sins year by year (v. 3)

iii.   The assertion restated: It is impossible for the blood of bulls and goats to take away sins (v. 4)

b.   *The inspired testimony to a submissive Savior and His sufficient sacrifice (v. 5-10)*

i.   The inspired testimony of Messiah from Psalm 40:6-8 (v. 5-7)

ii.   The inspired exposition of Psalm 40:6-8 in light of the argument concerning the Old and New Covenant (v. 8-9)

iii.   The inspired declaration of the sufficiency of Christ's sacrifice— we have been sanctified once for all (v. 10)

4. The nullification of any need for further sacrifice for sins—because Christ has sanctified [perfected for all time] His people, and their sins are remembered no more (10:11-18)

    a.   The contrast between the Old Covenant priests and Christ (v. 11-14)

        i.   The Scripture's teaching concerning Old Covenant priests (v. 11)

        ii.   The Scripture's teaching concerning our New Covenant priest (v. 12-13)

        iii.   The superior ministry of Christ as high priest summarized (v. 14)

    b.   The confirmation of the Spirit-inspired Scriptures—that New Covenant believers are complete by what Christ has done (v. 15-17)

        i.   The witness of the Holy Spirit concerning the New Covenant (v. 15)

        ii.   The work of God in the heart promised in the New Covenant (v. 16)

        iii.   The wonder of forgiveness promised in the New Covenant (v. 17)

    c.   The conclusion of the matter—there is no longer any offering for sin (v. 18)

[D. **WARNING #4: The New Covenant access we have compels us to hold fast to Christ and endure in the faith (10:19-39)**[*]

    1. Let us draw near, hold fast, and encourage one another in the sufficiency of Christ (10:19-25)

        a.   Let us draw near to God in worship (v. 19-22)

            i.   The confidence to draw near (v. 19-21)

                aa.   Christ's passion gives us direct access to God (v. 19-20)

                bb.   Christ's priesthood gives Him authority over the house of God (v. 21)

            ii.   The command to draw near (v. 22)

                aa.   With a sincere heart

                bb.   In full assurance of faith

                cc.   Having been made clean

        b.   Let us hold fast the confession of our hope (v. 23)

            i.   The confession of our hope

            ii.   The confidence of our hope

        c.   Let us encourage one another to love and good deeds (v. 24-25)

            i.   Discover how to stir one another up (v. 24)

---

[*] alternate outline depending on the division of the text. These points are perhaps better under the next section.

ii.   Do not forsake assembling together (v. 25)

2. Let us consider the consequences of rejecting Christ (10:26-31)

    a. *If you reject New Covenant access through Christ, there no longer remains a sacrifice for sins (v. 26-27)*

        i.   If you reject the New Covenant perspective of Christ, there is no propitiation for sins (v. 26)

        ii. If you reject the New Covenant perspective of Christ, there is only punishment (v. 27)

    b. *If you reject New Covenant access through Christ, the punishment is infinitely more severe than disregarding the Old Covenant Law of Moses (v. 28-31)*

        i.   Anyone who rejects the Old Covenant Law of Moses dies without mercy (v. 28)

        ii. How much severe punishment is deserved for rejecting New Covenant grace found in the Son of God? (v. 29-31)

            aa. The question of rejecting God's Son, God's blood, and God's grace (v. 29)

            bb. The quotations concerning God's perfect judgment (v. 30)

            cc. The comparison—human justice is temporal, but divine justice is eternal (v. 31)

3. Let us endure in the faith (10:32-39)]

Part Three—New Covenant Faith in Jesus, the Son of God, is the Only Acceptable Way to Worship God (10:19-13:25)

I. Let us draw near, hold fast, and encourage one another in the sufficiency of Christ (10:19-25)

A. Let us draw near to God in worship (10:19-22)

1. The confidence to draw near (10:19-21)

    a. *Christ's passion gives us direct access to God (v. 19-20)*

    b. *Christ's priesthood gives Him authority over the house of God (v. 21)*

2. The command to draw near (10:22)

    a. *With a sincere heart*

    b. *In full assurance of faith*

    c. *Having been made clean*

B. Let us hold fast the confession of our hope (10:23)

1. The confession of our hope

2. The confidence of our hope

C. **Let us encourage one another to love and good deeds (10:24-25)**

    1. Discover how to stir one another up (10:24)

    2. Do not forsake assembling together (10:25)

II. **WARNING #4: Let us consider the consequences of rejecting Christ and the New Covenant (10:26-39)**

A. **If you reject New Covenant access through Christ, there no longer remains a sacrifice for sins (10:26-27)**

    1. If you reject the New Covenant perspective of Christ, there is no propitiation for sins (10:26)

    2. If you reject the New Covenant perspective of Christ, there is only punishment (10:27)

B. **If you reject New Covenant access through Christ, the punishment is infinitely more severe than disregarding the Old Covenant Law of Moses (v. 28-31)**

    1. Anyone who rejects the Old Covenant Law of Moses dies without mercy (10: 28)

    2. How much severe punishment is deserved for rejecting New Covenant grace found in the Son of God? (10:29-31)

        a. The question of rejecting God's Son, God's blood, and God's grace (v. 29)

        b. The quotations concerning God's perfect judgment (v. 30)

        c. The comparison—human justice is temporal, but divine justice is eternal (v. 31)

C. **If you respond in faith and do not shrink back, there is great reward (10:32-39)**

    1. Remember what you have already endured (10:32-34)

        a. Being spiritually enlightened, you endured great suffering personally (v. 32-33a)

            i. The reason you endured (after being enlightened)

            ii. The recognition of the suffering (a great conflict of sufferings)

        b.   *Being spiritually enlightened, you identified yourself with others who suffered for the gospel (v. 33b-34)*

            i.   The recognition of the identification with those who suffered (v. 33b)

            ii.   The realities of the associated suffering (v. 34a)

            iii.   The reason you endured (v. 34b)

2. Retain your confidence and you will receive your reward (10:35-39)

        a.   *Remain confident in your faith for there is great reward (v. 35-36)*

            i.   The reward is for those who keep their confidence in Christ (v. 35)

            ii.   The reward comes after you have done the will of God (v. 36)

        b.   *Remember that Christ is coming and the just will live by faith (v. 37-38)*

            i.   The promised hope (v. 37)

            ii.   The proper response to the promise of God—trust (v. 38)

        c.   *Realize who you are as one who hopes in God's Word (v. 39)*

            i.   We are not of those who shrink back to destruction (v. 39a)

            ii.   We are of those who have faith to the preserving of the soul (v. 39b)

III. Let us remember those who endured in living by the faith (11:1-12:3)

A. The summary statement concerning living by faith (11:1-2)

1. Faith is the assurance and conviction of things promised, but not yet seen (11:1)

2. Faith issues in the approval of those who exercised it (11:2)

B. The survey of living by faith in the Old Testament (11:3-38)

1. Faith in the pre-flood era: From creation to Noah (11:3-7)

        a.   *Creation itself testifies that faith in the Word of God is not mere wishful thinking (v. 3)*

        b.   *Abel's sacrifice still speaks of genuine faith (v. 4)*

        c.   *Enoch was pleasing to God because of his faith (v. 5-6)*

        i.   Walking with God means trusting in Him (v. 5)

        ii.   Without faith it is impossible to please Him (v. 6)

    d.   *Noah was delivered from the condemnation of the world because of his faith (v. 7)*

2.   **Faith in the patriarchal era: From Abraham to Jacob (11:8-22)**

    a.   *By faith Abraham lived as stranger in this world (v. 8-10)*

        i.   He left the known to go the unknown (v. 8)

        ii.   He lived as an alien in a land of promise (v. 9)

        iii.   He looked to the heavenly city (v. 10)

    b.   *By faith Sarah received the ability to conceive (v. 11-12)*

        i.   Her ability to conceive was tied to faith (v. 11)

        ii.   Her faith was integral to the fulfillment of God's plan and promises (v. 12)

    c.   *Before receiving the fulfillment of all the promises, the patriarchs died in faith (v. 13-16)*

        i.   They lived as pilgrims (v. 13)

        ii.   They had a heavenly perspective (v. 14-16)

        iii.   They have the pride of God and a divinely prepared city (v. 15-16)

    d.   *By faith the patriarchs testified to their hope in the future fulfillment of God's promises (v. 17-22)*

        i.   Abraham offered Isaac and received him back (v. 17-19)

        ii.   Isaac blessed Jacob and Esau accordingly (v. 20)

        iii.   Jacob blessed Joseph's sons and worshipped (v. 21)

        iv.   Joseph testified of the exodus and through his funeral arrangements (v. 22)

3.   **Faith in the Mosaic era: From Moses' birth to the Exodus (11:23-29)**

    a.   *By faith Moses' parents had the courage to protect him in spite of Pharaoh's edict (v. 23)*

    b.   *By faith Moses had the courage to identify with the people of God rather than as a prince in Egypt (v. 24-26)*

       c.   *By faith Moses had the courage to lead the Exodus, keep the Passover,*
           and pass through the Red Sea (v. 27-29)

4.   Faith in the conquest and kingdom era: From Joshua to the prophets (11:30-38)

    a.   *By faith Jericho fell (v. 30)*

    b.   *By faith Rahab survived its fall (v. 31)*

    c.   *By faith Israel's heroes triumphed—in life and in death (v. 32-38)*

        i.   The notable names of faith (v. 32)

            aa. Gideon, Barak, Samson, Jephthah

            bb. David, Samuel, the prophets

        ii. The notable exploits of faith (v. 33-35a)

            aa. They conquered kingdoms by faith

            bb. They performed acts of righteousness by faith

            cc. They obtained promises by faith

            dd. They shut the mouths of lions by faith

            ee. They quenched the power of fire by faith

            ff.   They escaped the edge of the sword by faith

            gg. They were weak but were made strong by faith

            hh. They became mighty in war by faith

            ii.   They put foreign armies to flight by faith

            jj.   Women received back their dead through resurrection by faith

        iii. The nameless heroes who endured hardship by faith (v. 35b-38)

            aa. Some were tortured unto death

            bb. Some were mocked and beaten, chained and imprisoned

            cc. Some were executed

            dd. Some were destitute and afflicted

C. The summary statement concerning living faith *in the Old Testament era* (11:39-40)

1. Old Testament saints were justified by faith (11:39)

2. Old Testament saints will actually receive the ultimate fulfillment of God's promise because of the New Covenant that we have (11:40)

D. The specific application concerning living by faith in the New Testament era (12:1-3)

1. Let us continue in the life of faith (12:1-2)

   a. *Looking to the Old Testament examples of living by faith for encouragement (v. 1a)*

   b. *Laying aside everything that hinders you from living by faith (v. 1b)*

   c. *Looking specifically to Jesus for help to endure (v. 2)*

      i. He is the Source and Completer of faith

      ii. He is the ultimate example of living by faith

         aa. For the joy set before Him He endured the cross

         bb. After enduring in faith, He is exalted to the right hand of God

2. Let us consider especially the faith and endurance of Jesus (12:2-3)

   a. *He is the Source and Completer of faith (v. 2a)*

   b. *He is the ultimate example of and encouragement for living by faith (v. 2b-3)*

      i. For the joy set before Him He endured the cross

      ii. After enduring in faith, He is exalted to the right had of God

      iii. He endured persecution to the end

      iv. His example can encourage you not to grow weary and lose heart

IV. WARNING #5: Let us endure in our faith and embrace the discipline of the Lord—and let no one come short of the grace of God and refuse the Word of God (12:4-29)

A. Embrace the discipline of the Lord (12:4-11)

1. Regard faithfulness as more important than life/death (12:4)

2. Remember the exhortation of God concerning His sons (12:5-11)

   a. *The biblical citation concerning the Father's discipline (v. 5-6)*

   b. *The implications of fatherly discipline (v. 7-11)*

      i. It is to educate rather than punish (v. 7)

      ii. If you escape discipline you are not a son (v. 8)

      iii. If we respected the training of our earthly fathers, should we not all the more respect and receive the training of our heavenly Father? (v. 9-10)

      iv. If we allow ourselves to be trained by the Lord's discipline, it will reap the benefits of righteousness—even though it seems painful for the moment (v. 11)

B. Exercise your faith by pursuing holiness rather than temporary relief (12:12-17)

1. Stop being paralyzed and start walking by faith (12:12-13)

   a. *Straiten up (v. 12)*

   b. *Start walking by faith (v. 13)*

2. Seek the welfare of all men and the holiness that God calls you to (12:14)

3. See to it that none among you settle for temporary relief rather than the genuine grace of God (12:15-17)

   a. *The corporate responsibility: See to it that no one fails to embrace the grace of God (v. 15a)*

    b.   *The consequence of not guarding grace in the congregation: Seeking temporal relief rather than living by faith can have devastating results (v. 15b-17)*

        i.   The principle: An idolatrous person seeking temporary relief can defile many (v. 15b)

        ii.   The picture: Esau's choice of temporal relief rather than faith in the promise had lasting consequences (v. 16-17)

C. Express your gratitude for privilege of New Covenant worship by staying faithful to New Covenant worship (12:18-29)

   1. Worshipers under the New Covenant have a more fearful and glorious privilege than those of the Old Covenant (12:18-24)

      a.   *You have not come to an earthly representation of God's covenant dealings with man (v. 18-21)*

        i.   The place of the Old Covenant: Mt. Sinai (v. 18)

        ii.   The people of the Old Covenant and their response to hearing God (v. 19)

        iii.   The peculiar gravity of the Old Covenant manifestation of God (v. 20)

        iv.   The personal response of the mediator of the Old Covenant (v. 21)

      b.   *You have come to the heavenly reality of the New Covenant—which is the final expression of God's covenant dealings with man (v. 22-24)*

        i.   The superior place of the New Covenant (v. 22)

        ii.   The superior people of the New Covenant (v. 23)

        iii.   The superior Person/Mediator of the New Covenant (v. 24)

   2. Worshipers under the New Covenant have a more fearful and glorious accountability than those of the Old Covenant (12:25-29)

      a.   *The Old Covenant had earthly consequences—but the New Covenant has heavenly consequences (v. 25)*

      b.   *The Old Covenant came with an earthly earthquake—but the New Covenant will culminate in a cosmic/heavenly quake (v. 26-27)*

      c.   *The Old Covenant inaugurated a temporal kingdom—but the New Covenant is an eternal kingdom that cannot be destroyed (v. 28a)*

     d.   *Therefore, let us be thankful and respectful in our New Covenant service to God—because He is terrifyingly holy (v. 28b-29)*

V. Let us worship God by a life of faith (13:1-25)

A. The life of faith and the practice of love (13:1-6)

1. Keep on loving each other as brothers (13:1)

2. Keep on showing hospitality to strangers (13:2)

3. Keep on visiting those who are in chains (13:3)

4. Keep on honoring marriage and its sanctity (13:4)

5. Keep your character free from the love of money (13:5-6)

    a.   *The call for contentment (v. 5ab)*

    b.   *The confidence we have from Scripture (v. 5c-6)*

B. The life of faith and the practice of Old Covenant worship (13:7-16)

1. Be careful to follow leaders who accurately represented the word of God rather than strange doctrines (13:7-9)

    a.   *Be careful to follow those who accurately taught and lived the Word of God (v. 7)*

    b.   *Be confident that Jesus Christ does not change (v. 8)*

    c.   *Be careful to avoid those who teach strange doctrines that depart from grace (v. 9)*

2. Bear the reproach of Christ rather than go back to the Levitical system (13:10-16)

    a.   *Believers belong to a priesthood that far exceeds that of the Old Covenant (v. 10)*

    b.   *Believers are called to go outside the camp of Israel—bearing the reproach of Christ (v. 11-14)*

        i.   The Old Covenant sin offering that made atonement was burned outside the camp of Israel (v. 11; cf. Lev. 16)

        ii.   The New Covenant sin offering—Jesus—suffered outside the gate (v. 12)

      iii. The New Covenant believer must go outside the camp of Israel, bearing Christ's reproach (v. 13)

      iv. The New Covenant believer no longer seeks an earthly nationalism, but rather the future kingdom of God (v. 14)

    c. *Believers are called to offer up New Covenant sacrifices to God (v. 15-16)*

      i. A sacrifice of praise and thanksgiving (v. 15)

      ii. A sacrifice of doing good and sharing (v. 16)

C. The life of faith and the practice of fellowship (13:17-25)

1. Fellowship through submission to spiritual leadership (v. 17)

    a. *The command to obey and submit to spiritual leadership*

    b. *The care and concern spiritual leaders must have*

    c. *The cooperation required*

2. Fellowship through supplication for others (v. 18-19)

    a. *The prayer request made (v. 18)*

    b. *The powerful result expected (v. 19)*

3. Fellowship through the supplication of others (v. 20-21)

    a. *The Person addressed (v. 20)*

    b. *The prayer request (v. 21)*

4. Fellowship through submission to this epistle (v. 22)

5. Fellowship through straightforward statements of encouragement (v. 23-25)

    a. *Fellowship involves information and anticipation (v. 23)*

    b. *Fellowship involves affection (v. 24)*

    c. *Fellowship implies or expressly includes a benediction of grace (v. 25)*

James

Kress Biblical Resources

Overview Outline of James

Heavenly wisdom for persevering in your faith—even in the midst of severe trials (3:13-4:10)

I. Introduction (1:1)

   A.   The author

   B.   The audience

   C.   The address

II. Cling to God's wisdom in the midst of your trials, rather than your own (1:2-15)

   A.   Rejoice in the divine purpose of your trials (1:2-4)

   B.   Request divine wisdom to endure your trials with joy (1:5-8)

   C.   Remember that a poor believer has more to boast in than a rich man who only has his temporal possessions (1:9-11)

   D.   Recognize the purpose and source of your trials (1:12-15)

III. Cling to God's goodness and grace in the midst of your trials (1:16-18)

   A.   Cling to God's goodness (1:16-17)

   B.   Cling to God's grace (1:18)

IV. Concern yourself with obedience to God's Word in the midst of your trials (1:19-27)

   A.   Listen to God's Word rather than lash out in anger (1:19-21)

   B.   Live God's Word rather than merely hear it (1:22-27)

V. Cultivate genuine love, rather than favor the wealthy over the poor (2:1-13)

   A.   The precept: do not hold your faith with an attitude of personal favoritism (2:1)

   B.   The picture: two visitors—one dressed in fine clothes, the other dressed in dirty clothes (2:2-3)

   C.   The points to consider (2:4-13)

VI. Confess your faith by how you live—not just by what you say (2:14-26)

A. The proposition: faith without works is dead (2:14-17)

B. The proof: faith without works is dead (2:18-25)

C. The proposition restated: faith without works is dead (2:26)

VII. Control your tongue (3:1-12)

A. Consider the cost of becoming a teacher (3:1-2)

B. Consider the power of the tongue (3:3-12)

VIII. Check the fruit of your wisdom (3:13-18)

A. Behavior reveals the origin of your wisdom (3:13)

B. Bitter jealousy and selfish ambition characterize worldly, demonic wisdom (3:14-16)

C. Benevolence, righteousness, and peace characterize heavenly wisdom (3:17-18)

IX. Come to God in humility for the wisdom that produces divine peace (4:1-10)

A. Diagnose the source of conflicts among you (4:1-3)

B. Determine who you want to be your friend—the world or God (4:4-6)

C. Draw near to God in repentance and humility (4:7-10)

X. Control the urge to judge others (4:11-12)

A. The command: do not speak against one another (4:11a)

B. The consequences of not heeding the command: when you speak against others you are playing God (v. 11b-12)

XI. Consider your own plans as subject to divine change (4:13-17)

A. You do not know what your tomorrow holds (4:13-14)

B. You do know Who holds your tomorrow (4:15)

C. You demonstrate who you hold on to [trust in], by what you say and what you do (4:16-17)

XII. Consider the consequences of trusting in earthly riches (5:1-6)

A. Consider the sorrows of those who trust in earthly riches (5:1-3)

B. Consider the sins of those who trust in earthly riches (5:4-6)

XIII.Cultivate patient endurance as you wait for the Lord's return (5:7-11)

A. The precept: be patient until the coming of the Lord (4:7a)

B. The pictures: the farmer, the prophet, the patriarch Job (4:7b-11)

XIV.Carry all of life to the Lord in prayer (5:12-18)

A. Speak with integrity in every situation (5:12)

B. Seek the Lord in every situation (5:13-18)

XV.Correct the straying brother, and turn him back to the truth (5:19-20)

A. The caution: we are all prone to wander (4:19a)

B. The concern: we should seek to deliver a wandering brother (4:19b)

C. The consequences (4:20)

Introductory Matters

I. Introduction (1:1)

A. The author

1. Not likely the father of Judas (not Iscariot) mentioned only to distinguish his son from the other Judas (Luke 6:16, Acts 1:13)

2. Not likely James the son of Alpheus/James the less mentioned only in the lists of the Apostles (Matt. 10:3; Mark 3:18; Luke 6:1; cf. Matt. 27:65; Mark 15:40)

3. Not likely James the Son of Zebedee due to his early martyrdom around 44 AD (Acts 12:2)

4. James, the brother of Jesus according to the flesh

   a. *Skeptic and scoffer during Jesus' earthly ministry (John 7:5)*

   b. *Saved and saw the risen Christ (1 Cor. 15:7)*

   c. *Served as a notable leader, if not the leader of the early church*

      i.   Apostolic association (1 Cor. 15:7; Gal. 1:19; 2:9, 12 [notice James is mentioned first in 2:9])

      ii. Note Peter's designation by name (Acts 12:17)

      iii. Gave the final word and decision at Jerusalem council (Acts 15:13-19)

      iv. Even the Apostle Paul recognized and submitted to James's authority in matters of preference (Acts 21:17-26)

   d. *Slave of Jesus Christ (James 1:1)*

B. The audience

1. The original audience

   a. *Jewish believers scattered abroad (1:1)*

   b. *Struggling financially, facing various difficulties, including persecution for their faith (1:2-4, 9, 12; 2:6-7; 5:4-11; cf. Acts 8:1; 11:19)*

   c. *Struggling with significant internal conflict among their congregations (4:1-2, 11-12)*

2. The current audience

C. The aim

1. Encouragement to find joy in the Lord and persevere in the faith (1:1ff)

2. Edification in how to practically live out heavenly wisdom in the midst of life's trials (3:13-4:10 as the literary center of the epistle)

Detailed Outline of James

Heavenly wisdom for persevering in your faith—even in the midst of severe trials (3:13-4:10)

I. **Introduction (1:1)**

   A. **The author**

      1. His given name

      2. His glorious position

         a. *A slave of God*

         b. *A slave of the Lord Jesus Christ*

   B. **The audience**

      1. Who they were

      2. Where they were

   C. **The address**

II. **Cling to God's wisdom in the midst of your trials, rather than your own (1:2-15)**

   A. **Rejoice in the divine purpose of your trials (1:2-4)**

      1. The call you must heed—see trials as pure joy (v. 2)

      2. The concept you must embrace—knowing that trials produce endurance (v. 3)

      3. The constancy you must pursue—let endurance mature and perfect you (v. 4)

   B. **Request divine wisdom to endure your trials with joy (1:5-8)**

      1. God promises wisdom to the one who asks in faith (v. 5)

      2. God does not promise anything to the one who is double-minded about wanting to endure with joy (v. 6-8)

         a. *The prerequisite for receiving wisdom (v. 6a)*

         b. *The picture of one who wavers (v. 6b)*

         c. *The problem of having a divided mind (v. 7-8)*

C. Remember that a poor believer has more to boast in than a rich man who only has his temporal possessions (1:9-11)

   1. The lowly brother has an exalted position (v. 9)

   2. The wealthy man has only temporal possessions (v. 10-11)

      a. The irony: the rich man can only boast in what will end in humiliation (v. 10a)

      b. The illustration: a flower dries up and dies and has no lasting beauty (10b-11)

D. Recognize the purpose and source of your trials (1:12-15)

   1. The blessed purpose and result of testing is genuine faith and the crown of life (v. 12)

   2. The blameworthiness of temptation is not with God (v. 13)

   3. The bottom-line source of temptation is our own desire (v. 14)

   4. The birth of sin comes from pregnant desires that carry us away (v. 15)

III. Cling to God's goodness and grace in the midst of your trials (1:16-18)

A. Cling to God's goodness (1:16-17)

   1. Remember that you can be deceived by circumstances (v. 16)

   2. Remember that God is always good, in all things, at all times, in every way (v. 17)

B. Cling to God's grace (1:18)

   1. Remember God's grace in your personal salvation (v. 18a)

   2. Remember God's grace in the future salvation of a multitude (v. 18b)

IV. Concern yourself with obedience to God's Word in the midst of your trials (1:19-27)

A. Listen to God's Word rather than lash out in anger (1:19-21)

   1. Be quick to hear, slow to speak and slow to anger (v. 19)

   2. Be concerned about doing God's business, God's way (v. 20)

3. Be careful to repent of sin and receive the Word of God (v. 21)

B. Live God's Word rather than merely hear it (1:22-27)

1. The precept: live in light of the Word of God—and don't be deceived (v. 22)

2. The picture: look in the mirror and take to heart what you see (v. 23-24)

3. The prize: living in freedom of God's Word brings blessing (v. 25)

4. The points to consider: the freedom of God's Word limits your speech, enlivens your compassion, and excites your desire for holiness (v. 26-27)

V. Cultivate genuine love, rather than favor the wealthy over the poor (2:1-13)

A. The precept: do not hold your faith with an attitude of personal favoritism (2:1)

B. The picture: two visitors—one dressed in fine clothes, the other dressed in dirty clothes (2:2-3)

1. Two visitors in the assembly (v. 2)

2. Two very different responses (v. 3)

C. The points to consider (2:4-13)

1. Think about the previous illustration—you become a judge with evil motives (v. 4)

2. Think about God's general dealings with men—He exalts the lowly and rejects the proud (v. 5-7)

   a. *Does not God lavish grace on the poor who love and trust Him? (v. 5)*

   b. *Do you not recognize that you do the opposite when you dishonor the humble and pander to the proud who take advantage of you? (v. 6)*

   c. *Does it not bother you that the wealthy you are pandering to actually blaspheme Christ? (v. 7)*

3. Think about the benefits of mercy and love over human judgments (v. 8-13)

     a. Showing love always fulfills the law (v. 8)

     b. Showing partiality is sin and breaks the law (v. 9-11)

     c. So speak and act as a recipient of mercy, rather than a judge (v. 12-13)

VI. Confess your faith by how you live—not just by what you say (2:14-26)

A. The proposition: faith without works is dead (2:14-17)

1. The probing question: what use is it if someone says he has faith but he has no works? (v. 14)

2. The practical example: a brother without clothing and daily food (v. 15-16)

3. The plain statement of fact: faith, if it has no works, is dead (v. 17)

B. The proof: faith without works is dead (2:18-26)

1. A confession of faith is not necessarily proof of genuine faith (v. 18)

2. A confession of orthodoxy is not necessarily proof of genuine faith (v. 19-20)

     a. Demons have a measure of orthodoxy (v. 19)

     b. Do you recognize that faith without works is useless? (v. 20)

3. A consideration of two biblical examples confirms that genuine faith is vindicated by actions (v. 21-25)

     a. The faith of Abraham (the Father of the Jews) was vindicated by his deeds (v. 21-24)

       i. The rhetorical question posed (v. 21)

       ii. The relationship between faith and works explained (v. 22)

       iii. The results examined (v. 23-24)

     b. The faith of Rahab (a Gentile prostitute) was vindicated by her deeds (v. 25)

C. The proposition restated: faith without works is dead (2:26)

VII. Control your tongue (3:1-12)

   A. Consider the cost of becoming a teacher (3:1-2)

     1. Consider the caution, which is a command (v. 1a)

     2. Consider the concern of a stricter judgment and our propensity to stumble (v. 1b-2)

     3. Consider the control of the tongue as a sign of maturity (v. 2b)

   B. Consider the power of the tongue (3:3-12)

     1. The tongue is little, but incredibly powerful (v. 3-5)

       a. Contemplate the relationship between horse and bit (v. 3)

       b. Contemplate the relationship between rudder and ship (v. 4)

       c. Contemplate the relationship between the tongue and its talk—a forest fire and a spark (v. 5)

     2. The tongue is lethal (v. 6-8)

       a. The tongue is a deadly fire, which is ignited by hell itself (v. 6)

       b. The tongue is deadly predator, which cannot be tamed by the human race (v. 7-8)

     3. The tongue is linked to what is in your heart (v. 9-12)

       a. Consider the folly and hypocrisy of praise for God and the prideful cursing of men (v. 9-10)

         i. Praise for God (v. 9a)

         ii. Prideful cursing of men (v. 9b)

         iii. Plain hypocrisy (v. 10)

       b. Contemplate the fruit of your speech as an indicator of your heart (v. 11-12)

         i. A fountain can't send forth both fresh and bitter water (v. 11)

         ii. A fig tree can't produce olives and a vine cannot produce figs (v. 12a)

         iii. A foundational reality is that the source determines what is produced (v. 12b)

VIII. Check the fruit of your wisdom (3:13-18)

A. Behavior reveals the origin of your wisdom (3:13)

1. The rhetorical question about wisdom (v. 13a)

2. The revelation of true wisdom (v. 13b)

B. Bitter jealousy and selfish ambition characterize worldly, demonic wisdom (3:14-16)

1. Fallen wisdom is connected to jealousy, selfish ambition, and pride (v. 14)

2. Fallen wisdom is earthly, natural, demonic (v. 15)

3. Fallen wisdom results in disharmony and every evil thing (v. 16)

C. Benevolence, righteousness, and peace characterize heavenly wisdom (3:17-18)

1. God's wisdom is accompanied by the fruit of the Spirit (v. 17)

2. God's wisdom promotes righteousness and peace (v. 18)

IX. Come to God in humility for the wisdom that produces divine peace (4:1-10)

A. Diagnose the source of conflicts among you (4:1-3)

1. The source of conflicts introduced (v. 1)

2. The sequence of conflicts explained (v. 2ab)

3. The silence of God explained in regard to your desires (v. 2c-3)

B. Determine who you want to be your friend—the world or God (4:4-6)

1. Recognize your worldly affections (v. 4)

2. Realize that your worldly longings are not from God (v. 5)

3. Reconsider the truth of Proverbs 3:34 (v. 6)

C. Draw near to God in repentance and humility (4:7-10)

    1. Submit to God (v. 7a)

    2. Stand against the devil (v. 7b)

    3. Stay close to God (v. 8a)

    4. Scour your hands and hearts (v. 8b)

    5. Sorrow over your adulterous longings (v. 9)

    6. Stay low before God and He will exalt you (v. 10)

X. Control the urge to judge others (4:11-12)

A. The command: do not speak against one another (4:11a)

B. The consequences of not heeding the command: when you speak against others you are playing God (v. 11b-12)

    1. When you speak against your brother, you are speaking against God's law (v. 11b)

    2. When you speak against your brother, you set yourself in God's place (v. 12)

XI. Consider your own plans as subject to divine change (4:13-17)

A. You do not know what your tomorrow holds (4:13-14)

    1. The rebuke of presumption and self-reliance (v. 13)

    2. The reality about your knowledge of tomorrow (v. 14)

B. You do know Who hold your tomorrow (4:15)

C. You demonstrate who you hold on to [trust in], by what you say and what you do (4:16-17)

    1. Boasting in tomorrow's profit is evil (v. 16)

    2. Being silent about your reliance upon God is sin (v. 17)

XII. Consider the consequences of trusting in earthly riches (5:1-6)

A. Consider the sorrows of those who trust in earthly riches (5:1-3)

1. There will be future miseries (v. 1)

2. There will be the failure of earthly riches (v. 2-3a)

3. There will be the final judgment (v. 3b)

B. Consider the sins of those who trust in earthly riches (5:4-6)

1. Withholding pay from those it is due (v. 4)

2. Walking in wanton pleasure (v. 5)

3. Willful perversion of justice (v. 6)

XIII. Cultivate patient endurance as you wait for the Lord's return (5:7-11)

A. The precept: be patient until the coming of the Lord (4:7a)

B. The pictures: the farmer, the prophet, the patriarch Job (4:7b-11)

1. Patiently wait for the fruit of your labors, like the farmer (v. 7b-8)

   a. *A farmer must patiently wait for the fruit (v. 7b)*

   b. *A follower of Jesus must patiently await His coming (v. 8)*

2. Patiently wait for the vindication of the divine judge, like the prophets (v. 9-10)

   a. *Forsake complaining against one another—the divine Judge is coming (v. 9)*

   b. *Follow the example of the prophets who patiently endured suffering, waiting for the Lord's vindication (v. 10)*

3. Patiently wait for the Lord's consolation, like the patriarch Job (v. 11)

XIV. Carry all of life to the Lord in prayer (5:12-18)

    A. Speak with integrity in every situation (5:12)

    B. Seek the Lord in every situation (5:13-18)

        1. Pray when you are suffering (v. 13a)

        2. Praise God in song when you feel good (v. 13b)

        3. Pursue prayer in times of spiritual weakness or sin (v. 14-16ab)

            a. Call for the elders to pray if you feel too weak to pray for yourself (v. 14-15)

            b. Confess your sins to one another and pray for one another (v. 16ab)

        4. Pray knowing that prayer is unbelievably powerful (v. 16c-18)

            a. The bold statement—prayer is exceedingly powerful (v. 16a)

            b. The biblical support—Elijah (v. 17-18)

                i. Elijah's person (v. 17a)

                ii. Elijah's prayer (v. 17b-18)

XV. Correct the straying brother, and turn him back to the truth (5:19-20)

    A. The caution: we are all prone to wander (4:19a)

    B. The concern: we should seek to deliver a wandering brother (4:19b)

    C. The consequences (4:20)

        1. Salvation will be mediated (v. 20a)

        2. Sins will be covered (v. 20b)

1 Peter

Kress Biblical Resources

<u>Overview Outline of 1 Peter</u>

Standing firm in the true grace of God.

Part One—The True Grace of God is Given in Your Salvation (1:1-2:10)

I. The Gift and Greatness of Your Faith and Salvation (1:1-1:12)

A. Take comfort in God's election/choice (1:1-2)

B. Praise God for the basis and benefits of your faith and salvation (1:3-5)

C. Rejoice even in the testing of your faith and salvation (1:6-9)

D. Understand the glory and grandeur of your New Testament faith and salvation (1:10-12)

II. The Practice and Purpose of Your Faith and Salvation (1:13-2:12)

A. Your salvation calls you to focus your hope (1:13)

B. Your salvation calls you to holiness (1:14-16)

C. Your salvation calls you to godly fear [reverence/awe/respect] (1:17-21)

D. Your salvation calls you to love the brethren (1:22-25)

E. Your salvation calls you to crave God's Word (2:1-3)

F. Your salvation calls you to a new purpose: The worship of God (2:4-10)

Part Two—The True Grace of God is seen in Your Submission (2:11-3:12)

I. Submission to your calling and purpose (2:11-12)

A. You must wage war against sin and pursue righteousness (v. 11-12a)

B. You must make peace with who you are and why you are here (v. 11-12)

II. Submission to civil authority (2:13-17)

A. To whom are we to submit? (v. 13-14)

B. What are the motives for our submission? (v. 13-16)

C. How can we live out this submission? (v. 16-17)

III. Submission in society (2:18-25)

A.   Submission is inextricably bound to our relationship with God (v. 18b, 19b, 21a)

B.   Submission should not be biased by how we are treated (v. 18)

C.   Submission is beautiful to God (v. 19-20)

D.   Submission is based on the Person and work of Jesus Christ (v. 21-25)

IV. Submission in the home (3:1-7)

A.   The wife's role (v. 1-6)

B.   The husband's role (v. 7)

V. Submission in summary/general (3:8-12)

A.   Your submission will be evident in your selfless attitudes—especially toward the church (3:8)

B.   Your submission will be evident in your selfless actions—especially in response to unjust hostility (3:9a)

C.   Your submission is part of your calling—it brings blessing and intimacy with God (3:9b-12)

Part Three—The True Grace of God Sustains You in Your Suffering (3:13-5:14)

I.   The true grace of God (your hope of glory) compels you to entrust your soul to God's perfect will in suffering for righteousness [Things to remember when faced with suffering for righteousness] (3:13-4:19)

A.   You must understand the will of God in relation to suffering for doing what is right (3:13-17)

B.   You must look at the glorious results of Christ's suffering [according to the will of God] in the midst of your suffering for doing what is right (3:18-22)

C.   You must decidedly live for the will of God, even if it means suffering unto death for doing what is right (4:1-6)

D.   You must actively pursue ministry, love and the glory of God in the midst of your suffering for doing what is right, because the end is near (4:7-11)

E.   You must persevere and commit yourself to God in the midst of your suffering for doing what is right (4:12-19)

II. The true grace of God (your hope of glory) equips you for victory in the spiritual battle involved in suffering (5:1-14)

A. The true grace of God (your hope of glory) should govern your relations with other believers in light of the spiritual battle and suffering (5:1-5)

B. The true grace of God (your hope of glory) should govern your attitudes in the midst of the spiritual battle and suffering (5:6-11)

C. The true grace of God (your hope of glory) is able to make you stand firm (5:12-14)

Introductory Matters

I. The author

A. The human author

1. Peter (1:1)

2. An Apostles (1:1)

3. A fellow elder (5:1)

4. A witness of the sufferings of Christ (5:1)

5. A partaker also of the glory that is to be revealed (5:1)

B. The divine Author (2 Tim. 3:16-17; 2 Pet. 1:20-21)

II. The audience

A. The original recipients

1. Elect sojourners (1:1)

2. Scattered in Asia minor (1:1)

3, Jewish and perhaps a mixture of Gentile believers (1:8; 2:10; 4:3-4)

4. Facing severe suffering and persecution (1:6-7; 2:19-21; 3:14, 17; 4:1, 12-16, 19; 5:8-10)

B. The current recipients (2 Tim. 3:16-17; cf. Rom. 15:4; 1 Cor. 10:11)

III. The Reasons

A. To encourage believers in their salvation (1:1-2:10)

B. To encourage believers to testify of their salvation through submission (2:11-3:12)

C. To encourage believers to endure in the face of suffering (3:13-5:14)

D. Summary: To encourage believers to stand firm in the true grace of God—no matter the opposition (5:10-12)

Detailed Outline of 1 Peter

Standing firm in the true grace of God.

Part One—The True Grace of God is Given in Your Salvation (1:1-2:10)

I. **The Gift and Greatness of Your Faith and Salvation (1:1-1:12)**

   A. **Take comfort in God's election/choice (1:1-2)**

      1. Be encouraged in God's choice of Peter as the human author (1:1a)

      2. Be encouraged in God's choice of believers as elect aliens (1:1-2c)

         a. *Chosen homeless according to the foreknowledge of God the Father (v. 1-2a)*

         b. *Chosen homeless by the sanctifying work of God the Holy Spirit (v. 2b)*

         c. *Chosen homeless for the purpose of obedience and the cleansing of God the Son (v. 2c)*

      3. Be encouraged in God's choice of greetings in this epistle (1:2c)

   B. **Praise God for the basis and benefits of your faith and salvation (1:3-5)**

      1. Praise Him for the basis of your faith and salvation (v. 3)

         a. *His great mercy*

         b. *His power through resurrection of Jesus Christ*

      2. Praise Him for the benefits of your faith and salvation (v. 3-5)

         a. *A living hope (v. 3)*

         b. *A lavish and indestructible inheritance (v. 4)*

            i. Imperishable

            ii. Undefiled

            iii. Unfading

iv.   Reserved in heaven

    c.   A lasting and powerful protection unto salvation (v. 5)

C.   Rejoice even in the testing of your faith and salvation (1:6-9)

1.   Rejoice in the basis and benefits of your faith and salvation (v. 6a)

2.   Rejoice in the refining of your faith and salvation (v. 6-7)

    a.   Remember it is only for a little while (v. 6b)

    b.   Remember it is only if God deems it necessary (v. 6c)

    c.   Remember proven faith results in reward (v. 7)

3.   Rejoice in the Object of your faith, Who is your salvation (v. 8)

4.   Rejoice in the outcome of your faith: Salvation (v. 9)

D.   Understand the glory and grandeur of your New Testament faith and salvation (1:10-12)

1.   The Old Testament prophets longed to understand what you understand about salvation (v. 10-12a)

    a.   They studied the gospel in an inspired Old Testament [including their own writings] (v. 10-11)

      i.   They sought to understand more clearly the future plan of God's redeeming grace (v. 10) [cf. Jn. 1:16-17 "grace and truth were realized through Jesus Christ"]

      ii.   They sought to understand more clearly the sufferings of Messiah [The incarnation and crucifixion of Jesus Christ] (v. 11a)

      iii.   They sought to understand the future glories of Messiah [The resurrection, ascension, exaltation and glorious return of Jesus Christ] (v. 11b)

    b.   They saw their predictive ministry as serving primarily New Testament believers (v. 12a)

2.   The angels long to understand what you understand about salvation (v. 12b)

II. The Practice and Purpose of Your Faith and Salvation (1:13-2:12)

A. Your salvation calls you to focus your hope (1:13)

1. Purpose once and for all to be prepared mentally [to think biblically about life in light of Christ's return]

2. Perpetually [continually] control your thinking

3. Be pre-occupied with the glory to come

B. Your salvation calls you to holiness (1:14-16)

1. You must continually wage war against sin in your life (v. 14)

   a. *Remember who you are now—children of obedience (v. 14a)*

   b. *Remember who you were—ignorant slaves to sin (v. 14b)*

2. You must clearly seek to reflect the holy character of God (v. 15-16)

   a. *Remember: God is the standard of holiness (v. 15a)*

   b. *Remember: God is concerned with every area of your life (v. 15b)*

   c. *Remember: God's Word commands it (v. 16)*

C. Your salvation calls you to godly fear [reverence/awe/respect] (1:17-21)

1. Remember who God is [and what He is doing] (v. 17)

   a. *He is Father*

   b. *He is Judge*

2. Remember what God has done in Christ (v. 18-21)

   a. *He paid an infinitely costly price to redeem you (v. 18-19)*

      i. Not redeemed with human treasure (v. 18a)

      ii. Redeemed from slavery to sin (v. 18b)

      iii. Redeemed by the life-blood of the sinless Christ (v. 19)

   b. *He has given you faith and hope (v. 20-21)*

      i. Based on an eternal plan of redemption (v. 20a)

      ii. Through the incarnation of God for you (v. 20b)

      iii. Because of the resurrection and ascension of Christ (v. 21)

D. Your salvation calls you to love the brethren (1:22-25)

1. The prerequisite of love for the brethren: Obedience to the soul-cleansing truth of God's Word (v. 22a)

2. The manner of love for the brethren (v. 22b)

    a.   *Unhypocritical, brother-love/affectionate love*

    b.   *Fervent, sacrificial love from the heart*

3. The reasons for love of the brethren (v. 22-25)

    a.   *Because we are commanded to (v. 22)*

    b.   *Because we share the same eternal life-blood/new birth (v. 23-25)*

        i.   We have the same life-giving, imperishable seed, which is the source of our new birth (v. 23a)

        ii.   We were made alive through the same living and abiding Word of God, which is the means of our new birth (v. 23-25)

            aa.   Scripture says that everything else is temporal (v. 24)

            bb.   Scripture also says that God's Word is eternal (v. 25a)

            cc.   We heard God's Word as good news preached to us (v. 25b)

E. Your salvation calls you to crave God's Word (2:1-3)

1. Learn to appreciate the power and abiding value of God's Word (v. 1a; "Therefore")

2. Lay aside sin, which hinders desire for God's Word (v. 1b)

    a.   *All malice*

    b.   *All deceit*

        i.   Including hypocrisies

        ii.   Including envy

    c.   *All slander*

3. Liken God's Word to your only source of life (v. 2a)

4. Lean on God's Word as your most essential means of growth (v. 2b)

5. Love the One revealed in God's Word as good and gracious (v. 3)

F. Your salvation calls you to a new purpose: The worship of God (2:4-10)

1. Worship Part I: Being built up as a new temple, for new priesthood and new sacrifices (v. 4-8)

   a. *Worship because of who you are in Christ (v. 4-8)*

      i. Those who come to Christ as the only living, God-ordained foundation (v. 4)

      ii. Those who are living stones, in a new temple, with a new priesthood, and new sacrifices (v. 5)

      iii. Those who are believers in Christ as the predicted cornerstone (v. 6)

      iv. Those who are in contrast to disobedient, stumbling, rejecters (v. 7-8)

   b. *Worship because of what God has accomplished for us in Christ (v. 4-8)*

      i. God has made your worship acceptable to Him through Christ (v. 4-5)

      ii. God has guaranteed no shame or disappointment for believers in Christ (v. 6)

      iii. God has given you the only sure foundation to build your life upon (v. 7)

   c. *Worship because God in Christ is supremely worthy (v. 4-8)*

      i. Christ is alive from the dead (v. 4a)

      ii. Christ is elect and precious in God's sight (v. 4b)

      iii. Christ is able to make your worship acceptable (v. 5)

      iv. Christ is the precious and divine Object of saving faith (v. 6)

      v. Christ is the sovereign judge of the disobedient (v. 7-8)

2. Worship Part II: Proclaiming His excellencies as the new people of God (v. 9-10)

    a.   Because of who we are in Christ

    b.   Because of what God has done for us in Christ

    c.   Because of who God is in Christ: He is worthy

Part Two—The True Grace of God is seen in Your Submission (2:11-3:12)

I. Submission to your calling and purpose (2:11-12)

  A. You must wage war against sin and pursue righteousness (v. 11-12a)

    1. War against sin (v. 11)

    2. Pursue righteousness (v. 12)

  B. You must make peace with who you are and why you are here (v. 11-12)

    1. Make peace with who you are (v. 11)

    2. Make peace with why you are here (v. 12)

II. Submission to civil authority (2:13-17)

  A. To whom are we to submit? (v. 13-14)

  B. What are the motives for our submission? (v. 13-16)

    1. For the Lord's sake

      a.   God commands it

      b.   Jesus submitted to civil authority

      c.   Submission brings God glory

    2. For such is the will of God

  C. How can we live out this submission? (v. 16-17)

    1. Remember that you're free (v. 16)

    2. Honor all men

3. Love the brotherhood

4. Fear God

5. Honor the king

III. Submission in society (2:18-25)

A. Submission is inextricably bound to our relationship with God (v. 18b, 19b, 21a)

1. Because of the fear/respect of God (v. 18b)

2. Because of the consciousness of God (v. 19b)

3. Because of the conversion/call of God (v. 21a)

B. Submission should not be biased by how we are treated (v. 18)

C. Submission is beautiful to God (v. 19-20)

D. Submission is based on the Person and work of Jesus Christ (v. 21-25)

1. Christ's example (v. 21-23)

   a. *His suffering left a pattern for us to follow (v. 21b)*

   b. *His suffering was undeserved (v. 22)*

      i. He was sinless in conduct

      ii. He was sinless in His words (cf. James 3:2)

   c. *His suffering did not lead him to retaliation [in word or deed] (v. 23)*

   d. *His suffering revealed His faith [He entrusted all things to Him who judges righteously] (v. 23b)*

2. Christ's redemption/atonement (v. 24-25)

   a. *He is our Substitute (v. 24)*

      i. How?

      ii. For what purpose?

   b. *He is our Savior (v. 24c)*

      i. His wounds

      ii. Our healing

  c. *He is our Shepherd (v. 25)*

    i. Our waywardness

    ii. Our repentance

    iii. His authority and care

IV. Submission in the home (3:1-7)

A. The wife's role (v. 1-6)

 1. Pursue submissive and respectful behavior (v. 1-2)

  a. To her own husband (v. 1a)

  b. Even if her husband is disobedient to God's Word (v. 1b)

  c. For the sake of God's glory and her husband's good (v. 1c-2)

 2. Pursue modesty in external adornment (v. 3)

 3. Pursue beauty that will never perish (v. 4-6)

  a. Remember what is precious/beautiful to God (v. 4)

  b. Remember the godly women of the Old Testament (v. 5-6a)

    i. The general example of those holy women who hoped in God (v. 5)

    ii. The specific example of Sarah (v. 6a)

  c. Remember the assurance that comes from doing what is right in faith (v. 6b)

B. The husband's role (v. 7)

 1. Actively seek a home that reveals your hope in God [likewise] (v. 7a; cf. 2:11-12)

 2. Actively seek to understand your wife (v. 7b)

 3. Actively seek to honor your wife (v. 7c)

  a. In light of her relationship with God

  b. In light of your relationship with God

V. Submission in summary/general (3:8-12)

A. Your submission will be evident in your selfless attitudes—especially toward the church (3:8)

1. Like-mindedness

2. Sympathy

3. Brotherly love

4. Compassion

5. Humility

B. Your submission will be evident in your selfless actions—especially in response to unjust hostility (3:9a)

1. Not returning evil for evil

2. But giving a blessing in the face of evil

C. Your submission is part of your calling—it brings blessing and intimacy with God (3:9b-12)   ·

1. The principle stated (3:9b)

2. The Scriptural basis (3:10-12)

   a.   *The desire for blessing (v. 10a)*

   b.   *The requirement of a submissive life (v. 10b-11)*

   c.   *The LORD's response to all men (v. 12)*

Part Three—The True Grace of God Sustains You in Your Suffering (3:13-5:14)

I. **The true grace of God (your hope of glory) compels you to entrust your soul to God's perfect will in suffering for righteousness [Things to remember when faced with suffering for righteousness] (3:13-4:19)**

   A. **You must understand the will of God in relation to suffering for doing what is right (3:13-17)**

      1. You will not normally [or ultimately—cf. v. 12] suffer for doing what is right [it is not God's original design for mankind, or His usual way of governing the universe] (3:13)

      2. You are blessed if you suffer for doing what is right (3:14a)

      3. You must fight the fear of man when you suffer for doing what is right (3:14b)

      4. You must cherish Christ above all else even when you suffer for doing what is right (3:15-16)

         a. *In private devotion [in your hearts] (v. 15a)*

         b. *In public witness (v. 15b)*

            i. At all times

            ii. With words of hope that can be biblically defended

            iii. In front of anyone

            iv. In a spirit of gentleness and reverence

         c. *In practical holiness: With a good conscience and godly life (v. 16)*

      5. You must understand God's sovereignty when you suffer for doing what is right (3:17)

   B. **You must look at the glorious results of Christ's suffering [according to the will of God] in the midst of your suffering for doing what is right (3:18-22)**

      1. The foundational truths of Christ's sufferings (v. 18)

         a. *Sympathetic High Priest [also]*

         b. *Sinless, substitionary death*

      c. Salvation—complete and final

2. The fruit of Christ's sufferings (v. 18-21)

    a. Victory over death in the spiritual and physical realm (v. 18)

    b. Vindication of God's plan in the demonic realm (v. 19-20)

    c. Verification of salvation in the human realm (v. 20-21)

3. The final outcome of Christ's sufferings—exaltation in the heavenly realm (v. 22)

C. You must decidedly live for the will of God, even if it means suffering unto death for doing what is right (4:1-6)

1. Because Christ viewed obedience to God's will as of much greater importance than His suffering unto death (v. 1a)

2. Because the one who is committed to God's will, even in suffering unto death, has broken free from sin's control (v. 1b-3)

    a. Perfect freedom from sin's control ultimately: Suffering unto death brings a perfect release from sin (v. 1b)

    b. Practical freedom from sin's control now (v. 2-3)

       i. God's will is now more important than the lusts of men (v. 2)

      ii. Pagan pursuits are now a thing of the past (v. 3)

         aa. Sensuality

         bb. Lusts

         cc. Drunkenness

         dd. Carousing

         ee. Drinking parties

         ff. Abominable idolatries

3. Because the one who is committed to God's will, even in suffering unto death, will be vindicated by God when He judges the living and dead (v. 4-6)

        a. *You may be maligned for your pursuit of holiness, but your accusers will answer to God (v. 4-5)*

            i. Your pursuit of holiness will bring a measure of conviction (v. 4a)

            ii. Your pursuit of holiness will elicit hostility from unbelievers (v. 4b)

            iii. Your accusers will have to give an account to the Judge of all the earth (v. 5)

        b. *You may be judged in death according to men, but the true Judge will give you life through the gospel (v. 6)*

D. You must actively pursue ministry, love and the glory of God in the midst of your suffering for doing what is right, because the end is near (4:7-11)

    1. Protect your mind for intimacy with God (v. 7)

        a. *Think clearly (v. 7a)*

        b. *Be alert (v. 7b)*

        c. *Unto prayer (v. 7c)*

    2. Purpose to actively love one another in the body of Christ, especially through forgiveness and hospitality (v. 8-9)

        a. *Fervently love one another (v. 8a)*

        b. *Cover sins (v. 8b)*

        c. *Be hospitable to one another (v. 9)*

    3. Pursue service within the body of Christ (v. 10-11c)

        a. *Serve one another with your unique giftedness (v. 10-11b)*

            i. All of us are stewards of God's multifaceted grace (v. 10)

            ii. If you speak, do so as God would (v. 11a)

            iii. If you serve, do so in God's strength (v. 11b)

        b. *Serve one another with the purpose of glorifying God in all things (v. 11c)*

    4.   Praise and proclaim the glory and dominion of God in Christ as Peter did (v. 11d)

E. You must persevere and commit yourself to God in the midst of your suffering for doing what is right (4:12-19)

    1.   Realize the blessed purposes and results of being tested by fire [Expect testing to come to prove your faith] (v. 12)

        a.   Do not be surprised at the fiery ordeal among you (v. 12a)

        b.   It comes upon you for your testing (v. 12b)

        c.   It is not to be considered something alien to the Christian life (v. 12c)

    2.   Rejoice in the blessed fellowship of Christ's sufferings and the blessed hope of His return [Experience the joy of fellowship with Christ in both His suffering and His promised return] (v. 13)

        a.   The fellowship of Christ's sufferings (v. 13a)

        b.   The command to "keep on rejoicing" (v. 13b)

        c.   The result of rejoicing now, is exultation at Christ's return (v. 13b)

    3.   Revere/Respect the blessed Name of Christ [Exalt the Name of Christ above all else in your suffering] (v. 14-16)

        a.   If you're reviled for the Name of Christ, you are blessed (v. 14)

        b.   If you suffer in your in your own name—because of your own sin— there is cause for shame (v. 15)

        c.   If you suffer for the Name of Christ, you need not be ashamed, but rather glorify God in that Name (v. 16)

    4.   Receive God's blessed chastening now, instead of terrifying judgment later [Embrace God's chastening now, instead of eternal judgment later] (v. 17-18)

        a.   The refining judgment of the household of God (v. 17a)

        b.   The eternal judgment of those who do not obey the gospel of God (v. 17b)

        c.   The temporal difficulties of the righteous now (v. 18a)

        d.   The eternal difficulties of the godless and the sinner (v. 18b)

5.   Render yourself as wholly committed to the blessed will and authority of God as faithful Creator, and keep on doing what is right [Entrust yourself wholly to God's will and authority as faithful Creator, and keep on doing what is right] (v. 19)

II. **The true grace of God (your hope of glory) equips you for victory in the spiritual battle involved in suffering (5:1-14)**

A.   **The true grace of God (your hope of glory) should govern your relations with other believers in light of the spiritual battle and suffering (5:1-5)**

1.   Elders: Shepherd the flock of God (5:1-4)

a.   *Peter's example of hope-driven, gracious, voluntary oversight (v. 1)*

b.   *Peter's exhortation to hope-driven gracious, voluntary oversight (v. 2-4)*

i.   Shepherd willingly: Put away sloth (v. 2a)

ii.   Shepherd honestly: Put away greed (v. 2b)

iii. Shepherd humbly: Put away pride/lust for power (v. 3)

aa.   Not lording it over those allotted to your charge (v. 3a)

bb.   Proving to be examples to the flock (v. 3b)

iv.   Shepherd hopefully: Put away earthly motivations (v. 4)

aa.   When the Chief Shepherd appears (v. 4a)

bb.   You will receive the unfading crown of glory (v. 4b)

2.   Younger men: Be submissive to the elders (5:5a)

3.   All: Clothe yourselves with humility toward one another (5:5b)

B. The true grace of God (your hope of glory) should govern your attitudes in the midst of the spiritual battle and suffering (5:6-11)

1. Be submissive to the sovereignty of God (v. 6-7)

   a. *By remembering His character as revealed in the Scriptures (v. 6a-b)*

      i. He opposes the proud but gives grace to the humble [Therefore]

      ii. He is sovereign and all-powerful

   b. *By remembering the final outcome—exaltation (v. 6c)*

   c. *By remembering to cast your burden upon Him, because He cares for you (v. 7)*

2. Be sober and alert in view of the spiritual battle (5:8)

   a. *Know your responsibility*

      i. Be sober

      ii. Be watchful

   b. *Know your adversary*

      i. His character

      ii. His intent

3. Be strong in the Faith (5:9-11)

   a. *Know your responsibility (5:9a)*

   b. *Know you're not alone (5:9b)*

   c. *Know and rest in the promises, Person and praise of God (5:10-11)*

      i. The promises of God (v. 10)

         aa. Suffering for a little while

         bb. Eternal glory in Christ

         cc. Personal oversight of your perseverance and sanctification

      ii. The Person of God (v. 10)

         aa. The God of all grace

         bb. The God of sovereign grace

         cc. The God of eternal glory

  dd. The God of power and faithfulness (perfect, confirm, strengthen and establish you)

  iii. The praise of God (v. 11)

C. The true grace of God (your hope of glory) is able to make you stand firm (5:12-14)

1. Silvanus' ministry: Faithfulness and teamwork (5:12a)

2. Peter's ministry: The written Word of God—faithfulness to Christ's commission (5:12b)

3. The believer's charge: Stand firm in the true grace of God (5:12c)

4. The Church's wider ministry: Greetings of love (5:13-14a)

5. Christ's ministry: Peace to all who are in Him (5:14b)

2 Peter

Kress Biblical Resources

Overview Outline of 2 Peter

I. Introduction (1:1-2)

    A.   The writer (1:1a)

    B.   The recipients (1:1b)

    C.   The requisite greeting (1:2)

II. Remember the Word and be stirred up concerning your faith (1:1b, 3-21)

    A.   You've been given everything you need to live out your faith (1:1b, 3-4)

    B.   You have the responsibility to diligently live out your faith (1:5-11)

    C.   You have the truth of the Word of God to fortify and direct your faith (1:12-21)

III. Remember the Word and be stirred up concerning false teachers (2:1-22)

    A.   They will come—an introduction to the coming of false teachers (2:1-3a)

    B.   They will be condemned—an exposition of Old Testament examples of judgment and deliverance (2:3b-10a)

    C.   They will be corrupt in their character—an evaluation of who they really are (2:10b-22)

IV. Remember the Word and be stirred up concerning the future coming of Christ, and the coming day of judgment (3:1-16)

    A.   The truth of Christ's return and the judgment to come will be attacked by unbelievers with mocking and presumption (3:1-6)

    B.   The truth of Christ's return and the judgment to come is affirmed by God with His Word (3:7-10)

    C.   The truth of Christ's return and the judgment to come should be applied by believers with holiness of life (3:11-16)

V. Conclusion—guard against falling, but grow in grace (3:17-18)

    A.   Guard against error and against falling from your own steadfastness (3:17)

    B.   Grow in the grace and knowledge of our Lord and Savior Jesus Christ (3:18a)

    C.   Glory in Jesus Christ now and forever (3:18b)

Introductory Matters

I. Introduction (1:1-2)

A. The writer

1. The human author (1:1a)

    a. *His name*

    b. *His calling*

2. The divine author (1:12-21; cf. 2 Tim. 3:16-17)

B. The recipients (1:1b)

1. The original recipients (1:1b, 12, 20; 2:4-8, 15, 22; 3:15-16)

    a. *Believers [perhaps predominantly Gentile believers] (1:1b)*

    b. *Established in the truth (v. 12)*

    b. *Familiar with the Old Testament Scriptures (v. 20; 2:4-8, 15, 22)*

    c. *Recipients of the Apostle Paul's letters as Scripture (3:15-16)*

    d. *Facing the threat of false teachers/teaching (1:16a; 2:1ff; 3:3-4, 16)*

2. The current recipients

C. The reasons

1. Remember the Word, and be stirred up (1:12-15; 3:1)

2. Guard against falling from faithfulness into error (1:10, 19; 2:1ff; 3:17)

3. Grow in the grace and knowledge of our Lord and Savior Jesus Christ (1:2, 5-8; 3:14, 18)

4. In summary/outline form

    a. *Remember the Word and be stirred up concerning your <u>faith</u> (1:1-21)*

    b. *Remember the Word and be stirred up concerning <u>false teachers</u> (2:1-22)*

    b. *Remember the Word and be stirred up concerning the <u>future coming of Christ</u> (3:1-18)*

    c. *So that you may <u>guard</u> against falling into error; and <u>grow</u> in the grace and knowledge of our Lord and Savior, Jesus Christ (3:17-18)*

Detailed Outline of 2 Peter

I. **Introduction (1:1-2)**

   A. **The writer**

      1. The human author (1:1a)

         a. His name

         b. His calling

      2. The divine author (1:12-21; cf. 2 Tim. 3:16-17)

   B. **The recipients (1:1b)**

      1. The original recipients (1:1b, 12, 20; 2:4-8, 15, 22; 3:15-16)

         a. Believers [perhaps predominantly Gentile believers] (1:1b)

         b. Established in the truth (v. 12)

         c. Familiar with the Old Testament Scriptures (v. 20; 2:4-8, 15, 22)

         d. Recipients of the Apostle Paul's letters as Scripture (3:15-16)

         e. Facing the threat of false teachers/teaching (1:16a; 2:1ff; 3:3-4, 16)

      2. The current recipients

   C. **The requisite greeting (1:2)**

      1. The prayer for blessing

      2. The place/Person where that blessing is found

II. **Remember the Word and be stirred up concerning your faith (1:1b, 3-21)**

   A. **You've been given everything you need to live out your faith (1:1b, 3-4)**

      1. God's perfect provision is a gift of sovereign grace (1:1b, 3a)

         a. The gift of faith (v. 1b)

         b. The gift of every spiritual resource needed for life and godliness (v. 3a)

      2. God's perfect provision is backed by omnipotent power (1:3a)

      3. God's perfect provision has no limitation except God's life and likeness (1:3b)

4. God's perfect provision comes only through the true knowledge of Christ [i.e., the Word of God illumined to the true believer by the Holy Spirit] (1:3c)

5. God's perfect provision ensures your sanctification and victory over the world (1:4)

   a. *God's glory and excellence is the basis of your sanctification and victory*

   b. *God's gift is the source of your sanctification and victory*

   c. *God's nature (implanted by the Holy Spirit, through the Word of God) is the means of your sanctification and victory*

      i.   Believers partake of the divine nature

      ii. Believers escape the corruption that is in the world by lust

B. You have the responsibility to diligently live out your faith (1:5-11)

1. Faith in Christ lived out, culminates in spiritual character— i.e., love (1:5-7)

   a. *The basis for living out our faith in Christ (v. 5a)*

      i.   The divine nature and perfect provision given to us in the new birth

      ii. The divine command given to us, to live out our faith

      iii. The divine gift of faith

   b. *The basic ingredients of a faith that culminates in love (v. 5b-7)*

      i.   Moral excellence

      ii. Knowledge

      iii. Self-control

      iv. Perseverance

      v.   Godliness

      vi. Brotherly kindness

      vii. Love

2. Faith in Christ lived out, cultivates spiritual fruitfulness (1:8)

3. Faith in Christ lived out, conveys spiritual perception (1:9)

4. Faith in Christ lived out, confirms spiritual life (1:10-11)

  a. *The command to confirm your calling and election [assurance of salvation in time and eternity] (v. 10a)*

  b. *The confidence it brings now in the battle with sin [assurance of sanctification and perseverance now] (v. 10b)*

  c. *The confidence it brings concerning entrance into the eternal kingdom of our Lord and Savior Jesus Christ [assurance of glorification in the future] (v. 11)*

C. You have the truth of the Word of God to fortify and direct your faith (1:12-21)

1. The witness of this epistle is to be referenced repeatedly if we are to guard against error and grow in grace (1:12-15)

  a. *It was written to affirm foundational truths that relate to our faith (v. 12)*

  b. *It was written to arouse us from spiritual lethargy (v. 13-15)*

    i. He reminds us that it is right and needful to "be stirred up" in the faith (v. 13)

    ii. He reminds us that this world is not our home (v. 13a, 14, 15)

    iii. He reminds us that faithfulness is more important than death (v. 14-15)

  c. *It was written to aid/serve as a permanent reference for our faith (1:15)*

2. The witness of the Apostles (now contained in the New Testament) is to be trusted if we are to guard against error and grow in grace (1:16-18)

  a. It is based on fact, not fable (v. 16, 18)

  b. *It looks forward to the second coming of Christ (v. 16-17)*

  c. *It focuses on the majesty, honor and glory of Jesus Christ (v. 16-18)*

3. The witness of the prophetic word [the Old Testament as well as the rest of the Scriptures] is inspired by God and must be heeded if we are to guard against error and grow in grace until Christ comes (1:19-21)

    a.   The Scriptures are reliable—and self-confirming (v. 19a)

    b.   *The Scriptures are revealing—giving light in this dark and dreary world until Christ comes again (v. 19b)*

    c.   *The Scriptures are not a religion made by man—not a human interpretation of God, religion and history (v. 20)*

    d.   *The Scriptures are recorded by men, but in reality are the very Word of God—inspired by the Holy Spirit of God (v. 21)*

III. Remember the Word and be stirred up concerning false teachers (2:1-22)

A. They will come—an introduction to the coming of false teachers (2:1-3a)

1. Their arrival is assured (v. 1a)

2. Their doctrine will be destructive/damning (v. 1b)

3. Their example will be emulated by many (v. 2a)

4. Their ministry will misrepresent and malign the way of the truth (v. 2b)

5. Their purpose will be personal profit and self-promotion (v. 3a)

B. They will be condemned—an exposition of Old Testament examples of judgment and deliverance (2:3b-10a)

1. God's Word promises the condemnation of false teachers (2:3b)

2. God's Word pictures the condemnation of Old Testament proponents of false teaching, and the rescue of the righteous (2:4-10a)

    a.   *The condemnation of angels who sought to render mankind unredeemable (v. 4)*

    b.   *The condemnation of the antediluvian world, but the rescue of Noah and his family (v. 5) c.*   *The condemnation of Sodom and Gomorrah, but the rescue of Lot (v. 6-8)*

        i.   The destruction of Sodom and Gomorrah (v. 6)

        ii.   The deliverance of Lot (v. 7-8)

          aa.   The rescue (v. 7a)

          bb.   The reality of Lot's spiritual condition (v. 7-8)

    d.   *The certainty these examples bring that God knows how to rescue the godly and condemn the wicked (v. 9-10a)*

C. They will be corrupt in their character—an evaluation of who they really are (2:10b-22)

1. False teachers are full of arrogance and unsubmissive pride (2:10b-13a)

    a.   *They are self-willed instead of submissive (v. 10b-11)*

        i.   The crassness of their actions—they revile angelic majesties (v. 10b)

        ii.   The contrast of the angels—they do not revile angelic majesties (v. 11)

    b.   *They are senseless in their arrogance—and will ultimately reap what they sow (v. 12-13a)*

2. False teachers are full of avarice and ungodly passions (2:13b-16)

    a.   *Their shamelessness (v. 13b)*

    b.   *Their seductiveness (v. 14a)*

    c.   *Their selfish greed (14b-16)*

        i.   The fact (v. 14b)

        ii.   The false prophet Balaam (v. 15-16)

3. False teachers are full of false hope and emptiness, and are enslaved to sin (2:17-19)

    d.   *The false hope pictured (v. 17)*

        i.   Their deceptive appearance

        ii.   Their destruction

       e.   *The false hope promulgated (v. 18-19)*

           i.   Their deceptive words (v. 18-19a)

           ii.   Their destitute condition (v. 19b)

4.   False teachers are full of faithlessness, and are expressly unregenerate (2:20-22)

       a.   *Their tragic condition (v. 20)*

           i.   They knew the way of the truth

           ii.   They are overcome by corruption

           iii.   They are worse off than the common unbeliever

       b.   *Their terrifying culpability (v. 21)*

       c.   *Their true character (v. 22)*

IV. Remember the Word and be stirred up concerning the future coming of Christ, and the coming day of judgment (3:1-16)

A. The truth of Christ's return and the judgment to come will be attacked by unbelievers with mocking and presumption (3:1-6)

1.   Remember what the Word of God says (3:1-2)

       a.   *The letters of Peter (v. 1)*

       b.   *The Old Testament (v. 2a)*

       c.   *The New Testament (v. 2b)*

2.   Remember where mockers/unbelievers are coming from (3:3-6)

       a.   *They are slaves to their nature—mockers will mock, following after their own lusts (v. 3)*

       b.   *They are willfully ignorant of, and rebellious against the Word and power of God (4-6)*

           i.   They challenge God's promise (v. 4)

           ii.   They ignore God's power (v. 5-6)

                aa.   His power and authority in creation (v. 5)

                bb.   His power and authority in judgment (v. 6)

B. The truth of Christ's return and the judgment to come is affirmed by God with His Word (3:7-10)

   1. The day of Judgment is assured by divine power and promise (3:7)

       a. *Divine power*

       b. *Divine promise*

   2. The delay of judgment is on account of divine patience and timing (3:8-9)

       a. *Divine timing (v. 8)*

       b. *Divine patience and desire (v. 9)*

   3. The day of the Lord will arrive unannounced, with devastating destruction (3:10)

       a. *The surety of the day of the Lord*

       b. *The surprise of the day of the Lord*

       c. *The scourge of the day of the Lord*

C. The truth of Christ's return and the judgment to come should be applied by believers with holiness of life (3:11-16)

   1. We must live in light of the coming judgment (v. 11-12)

       a. *Holiness of life—consecration (v. 11)*

       b. *Hope—anticipation/expectation (v. 12)*

   2. We must live in light of the coming glory (v. 13-14)

       a. *The promise of the glory to come (v. 13a)*

       b. *The perfection of the glory to come (v. 13b)*

       c. *The peace, purity, and pursuit of blamelessness that results from expecting the glory to come (v. 14)*

   3. We must live in light of the current patience and grace of God (v. 15-16)

       a. *Regard the patience of our Lord as salvation (v. 15-16)*

          i. The command of Peter under the inspiration of the Spirit (v. 15a)

        ii.   The confirmation of Paul under the inspiration of the Spirit (v. 15b-16)

    b.   *Redeem the time of God's patience towards men (v. 15)*

    c.   *Refuse to distort the Scriptures—but rather be a faithful student (v. 16)*

V. Conclusion—guard against falling, but grow in grace (3:17-18)

A. Guard against error and falling from your own steadfastness (3:17)

1. Understand the Scriptures [that reveal God and His patience/salvation]

2. Understand the error of false teachers

3. Understand your own vulnerability

B. Grow in the grace and knowledge of our Lord and Savior Jesus Christ (3:18a)

1. The persistent pursuit of growth

2. The place of growth

3. The Person we look to as we grow

C. Glory in Jesus Christ now and forever (3:18b)

1 John

Kress Biblical Resources

Overview Outline of 1 John

Knowing you have fellowship with God and thus eternal life.

I. **Prologue: Eternal life is a reality—The Incarnation (1:1-4)**

   A.   The proclamation/message is true (1:1)

   B.   The Person is real (1:2)

   C.   The participation/fellowship is genuine (1:3)

   D.   The personal joy is unquestionable (1:4)

II. **God is Light: Possessors of eternal life have fellowship with the God Who is light (1:5-2:28)**

   A.   Possessors of eternal life walk in the light (1:5-7)

   B.   Possessors of eternal life confess sin (1:8-10)

   C.   Possessors of eternal life have the ultimate provision for sin (2:1-2)

   D.   Possessors of eternal life obey Christ's commandments (2:3-6)

   E.   Possessors of eternal life love other believers (2:7-11)

   F.   Possessors of eternal life have the foundation for a victorious life (2:12-14)

   G.   Possessors of eternal life do not ultimately love the world (2:15-17)

   H.   Possessors of eternal life believe the truth (2:18-28)

III. **God is Righteous: Possessors of eternal life have fellowship with the God Who is righteous (2:29-4:6)**

   A.   Possessors of eternal life practice righteousness (2:29)

   B.   Possessors of eternal life have the promised hope of ultimate righteousness (3:1-3)

   C.   Possessors of eternal life do not practice sin (3:4-10a)

   D.   Possessors of eternal life show themselves true by their love for the brethren (3:10b-24)

   E.   Possessors of eternal life can and must discern truth from error (4:1-6)

IV. God is Love: Possessors of eternal life have fellowship with the God Who is love (4:7-5:5)

A. Possessors of eternal life are compelled to love (4:7-12)

B. Possessors of eternal life can have assurance of a personal relationship with the God Who is love (mutual indwelling) (4:13-19)

C. Possessors of eternal life cannot separate love, faith, and obedience: They overcome the world (4:20-5:5)

V. God is Truth and Life: Possessors of eternal life have fellowship with the God Who is Truth and Life (5:6-21)

A. Possessors of eternal life believe God's testimony concerning His Son (5:6-12)

B. Possessors of eternal life have the certainty of eternal life and answered prayer (5:13-17)

C. Possessors of eternal life know the truth about their relationship to sin, the world, and God Himself (5:18-20)

D. Possessors of eternal life must guard themselves from idols (5:21)

Introductory Matters

I. Introduction

A. The author

1. The human author

    a. He was an eyewitness of Christ and the events of the gospel (1:1-3)

    b. He had definite, recognized authority among his audience (2:1, 7, 8, 15; 3:7, 18; 4:1-6))

    c. He employed grammar, style and vocabulary which are very similar to those same elements used by the author of the Gospel of John (cf. 1:4 with John 16:24; 4:6 with John 8:47; 5:12 with John 3:36)

2. The divine author (cf. 2 Tim. 3:16-17)

B. The audience

1. The original recipients

    a. Professing believers of all different maturity levels (2:1, 12-14)

    b. Perhaps a mainly non-Jewish audience, in that there are no direct quotations from the OT and very few allusions to it (3:12; see also 2:10-11; cf. Prov. 4:18-19)

    b. Facing the threat of false teachers and questions about truly possessing eternal life (2:26; cf. 2: 22-23; 4:2; see 5:13)

3. The current recipients

C. The aim

1. To bring fellowship with God through the apostolic witness (1:3)

2. To complete joy (1:4)

3. To encourage holiness (2:1)

4. To give encouragement and hope (2:12-14; cf. 2:1-2; 3:1-3; 4:4; 5:13)

5. To promote the assurance of eternal life (5:13)

D. The argument

Since true Christians have fellowship with God (1:3), they manifest the character of God and His Son Jesus Christ. First John says:

- God is light (1:5)

- God is righteous (2:29)

96

- God is love (4:7)

- God is truth and life (5:1, 6, 11, 12, 20)

Therefore, true Christians (possessors of eternal life) walk in the light, obey in righteousness and truth, live out love, and have eternal life. The reoccurring themes that depict genuine Christianity are *faith in the truth*, which produces *obedience to God's Word*, which leads to the *sacrificial love of the brethren*.

Detailed Outline of 1 John

Knowing you have fellowship with God and thus eternal life.

I. **Prologue: Eternal life is a reality—The Incarnation (1:1-4)**

   A. **The proclamation/message is true (1:1)**

   B. **The Person is real (1:2)**

   C. **The participation/fellowship is genuine (1:3)**

   D. **The personal joy is unquestionable (1:4)**

II. **God is Light: Possessors of eternal life have fellowship with the God Who is light (1:5-2:28)**

   A. **Possessors of eternal life walk in the light (1:5-7)**

      1. The foundation of our walk (1:5)

      2. The folly of empty talk (1:6)

      3. The freedom of our walk (1:7)

         a.   Freedom to live out truth and holiness

         b.   Freedom to enjoy fellowship

         c.   Freedom to experience constant cleansing

   B. **Possessors of eternal life confess sin (1:8-10)**

      1. The definition of biblical confession (Ps. 51; Ps. 5)

      2. The dominant reason why we confess sin (1:5, 8b, 10b)

      3. The description of those who don't confess sin (1:8, 10)

         a.   They deny sin

         b.   They are deceived

         c.   They are devoid of the truth

      4. The description of those who do confess sin (1: 9)

         a.   They are forgiven

         b.   They are cleansed

5. The declaration of God's character to those who confess sin (1:9)

   a. *He is faithful*

   b. *He is righteous*

C. Possessors of eternal life have the ultimate provision for sin (2:1-2)

1. Remember your responsibility to holiness (2:1a)

2. Remember your righteous Defender (2:1b)

3. Remember your righteous Defense (2:2)

D. Possessors of eternal life obey Christ's commandments (2:3-6)

1. The proof of fellowship comes by obedience (2:3)

2. The profession that is false is exposed by a lack of obedience (2:4)

3. The perfection of loves comes by obedience (2:5)

4. The picture of Christ is displayed by obedience (2:6)

E. Possessors of eternal life love other believers (2:7-11)

1. We are commanded to love (2:7, 8)

   a. *The old command*

   b. *The new command*

   c. *The biblical definition of love*

2. We are compelled to love [because of who we are] (2:8-11)

3. We are in contrast to those who walk in darkness (2:9-11)

F. Possessors of eternal life have the foundation for a victorious life (2:12-14)

   1. The fundamental foundation (2:12)

   2. The family framework of growth (2:12-14)

       a. *Fathers*

       b. *Young men*

       c. *Children*

   2. The Founder/Architect/Builder (2:12-14)

G. Possessors of eternal life do not ultimately love the world (2:15-17)

   1. Because it is commanded by God's Word (2:15a)

   2. Because of our love for the Father (2:15b)

   3. Because of all that is in the world and its opposition to God (2:16)

       a. *The lust of the flesh*

       b. *The lust of the eyes*

       c. *The pride of life*

   4. Because of our eternal perspective (2:17)

H. Possessors of eternal life believe the truth (2:18-28)

   1. The reason: Our anointing from the Holy One (2:20, 21, 27)

   2. The results (2:18-28)

       a. *We remain in the fellowship of believers (v. 18-19)*

       b. *We confess Christ (v. 22-23)*

       c. *We abide/remain in the true gospel (v. 24).*

       d. *We have the promise of eternal life (v. 25)*

       e. *We need not be deceived (v. 26-27)*

   3. The responsibility of believing the truth (2:28)

III. God is Righteous: Possessors of eternal life have fellowship with the God Who is righteous (2:29-4:6)

A. Possessors of eternal life practice righteousness (2:29)

1.   Because of our righteous God (2:29)

2.   Because of our new birth (2:29)

B. Possessors of eternal life have the promised hope of ultimate righteousness (3:1-3)

1.   The basis of our hope: The Father's love (3:1)

   a.   *God's love makes us children of God*

   b.   *God's love makes us strangers to the world*

2.   The future consummation of our Hope: Christ's coming (3:2)

3.   The present result of our hope: Personal purification (3:3)

C. Possessors of eternal life do not practice sin (3:4-10a)

1.   The reasons (3:4-9)

   a.   *Because of what sin is (v. 4)*

   b.   *Because of what Christ came to do and did (v. 5a, 8b)*

   c.   *Because of Who Christ is (v. 5b, 7)*

   d.   *Because of our relationship with Christ (v. 6)*

   e.   *Because of our new birth (v. 8a, 9)*

2.   The result: Our practice makes it obvious who we belong to (3:10)

D. Possessors of eternal life show themselves true by their love for the brethren (3:10b-24)

1.   It is a love that obeys God (3:10b-12)

   a.   *If you do not practice love, it testifies that you're not from God (v. 10b)*

   b.   *The command to love is inseparable from the gospel (v. 11)*

   c.   *Cain's murder of Abel was not from love—but an unbelieving response to God's love (v. 12)*

2.   It is a love that is foreign to this world (3:13-15)

    a.   *Love will often be met by hatred from this world [much like Cain's response to Abel] (v. 13)*

    b.   *Love of the brethren is an evidence of eternal life (v. 14-15)*

3.   It is a love that sacrifices for others (3:16-17)

    a.   *The perfect example of love for us to follow (v. 16)*

    b.   *The practice of love in everyday life (v. 17)*

4.   It is a love that shows in the sincerity of our lives (3:18)

5.   It is a love that brings assurance (3:19-24)

    a.   *Assurance that we are of the truth (v. 19-20)*

        i.   *Because we see evidences of God's love in our lives*

        ii.   *Because even when we fail in our love, God's love and understanding is greater than ours—which brings assurance*

    b.   *Assurance of confident access to God (v. 21-22)*

    c.   *Assurance of intimate union with God (v. 23-24)*

E.   Possessors of eternal life can and must discern truth from error (4:1-6)

1.   The command/warning to discern (4:1)

2.   The first test: Christological (4:2-3)

    a.   *The Spirit of God affirms the full humanity and full deity of Jesus Christ—the sufficiency of His Person and work (v. 2)*

    b.   *The spirit of antichrist denies the absolute sufficiency of Christ's Person and work (v. 3)*

3.   The assurance of victory (4:4)

4.   The second test: Bibliological (4:5-6)

    a.   *Those who reject the Apostles' teaching about Christ (v. 5)*

    b.   *Those who listen to the Apostles' teaching about Christ (v. 6)*

IV. God is Love: Possessors of eternal life have fellowship with the God Who is love (4:7-5:5)

  A. Possessors of eternal life are compelled to love (4:7-12)

    1. Because of Who God is (4:7-8)

    2. Because of what God has done in Christ (4:9-11)

       a. He has graciously revealed Himself (v. 9)

       b. He has mercifully atoned for sin (v. 10-11)

    3. Because of what God is doing in us (4:12)

  B. Possessors of eternal life can have assurance of a personal relationship with the God Who is love (mutual indwelling) (4:13-19)

    1. The basis for our assurance (4:13-16)

       a. The Holy Spirit (v. 13)

       b. Confirmed faith in the apostolic testimony of Christ (v. 14-15)

       c. Active love, which is based on faith in God (v. 16)

    2. The benefits of our assurance (4:17-18)

       a. Confidence in the day of judgment (v. 17)

       b. Freedom from fear (v. 18)

    3. The bottom line about love and assurance (4:19)

  C. Possessors of eternal life cannot separate love, faith, and obedience: They overcome the world (4:20-5:5)

    1. We cannot separate love from love (4:20-21)

    2. We cannot separate faith and love (5:1)

    3. We cannot separate love and obedience (5:2-3a)

    4. We cannot separate obedience and faith (5:3b-5)

V. God is Truth and Life: Possessors of eternal life have fellowship with the God Who is Truth and Life (5:6-21)

A. Possessors of eternal life believe God's testimony concerning His Son (5:6-12)

1. The testimony of history and the Holy Spirit (5:6-9)

   a. *The testimony history: Water and Blood (v. 6)*

   b. *The testimony of the Holy Spirit (v. 5-7)*

2. The internal testimony of eternal life (5:10)

3. The content of God's testimony (5:11)

4. The verdict (5:12)

B. Possessors of eternal life have the certainty of eternal life and answered prayer (5:13-17)

1. The certainty of eternal life (5:13)

   a. *The prerequisite*

   b. *The promise*

2. The certainty of answered prayer (5:14-16)

   a. *The promise (v. 14-15)*

   b. *The prerequisite (v. 14)*

   c. *The picture/illustration (v. 16a)*

   d. *The point of limitation (v. 16c)*

3. The certainty of the seriousness of sin (5:17)

C. Possessors of eternal life know the truth about their relationship to sin, the world, and God Himself (5:18-20)

1. We are no longer friends of sin (5:18)

2. We are no longer citizens of this world (5:19)

3. We are no longer estranged from God (5:20)

D. Possessors of eternal life must guard themselves from idols (5:21)

   1. What is an idol in the context of 1 John?

   2. How can we guard ourselves from idols?

2 John

Kress Biblical Resources

Overview Outline of 2 John

Living out love, in truth.

I. **The Truth Promotes Love—The Truth Issues in Love, Especially for Other Believers (v. 1-3)**

   A.   John's love (v. 1-2)

   B.   All believers' love (v. 1-2)

   C.   God's love (v. 3)

II. **Love promotes the truth (v. 4-11)**

   A.   Love rejoices in obedience to God's truth (v. 4)

   B.   Love is realized in obedience to God's Word of truth (v. 5-8)

   C.   Love does not receive or support those who contradict the truth about Christ (v. 9-11)

II. **Love and truth promote fellowship and joy (v. 12-13)**

   A.   True fellowship desires more than merely written communication (v. 12)

   B.   True fellowship produces fullness of joy (v. 12c)

   C.   True fellowship is based on God's sovereign grace (v. 13)

Introductory Matters

I. Introduction

A. The author

1. The human author

    a. His designation (v. 1a)

    b. His authority (v. 4-5, 8)

    c. His literary similarities to 1, 3 John and the Gospel of John

2. The divine author (cf. 2 Tim. 3:16-17)

B. The audience

1. The original recipients

    a. Believers (v. 1, 4)

    b. Possibly a house church (v. 10)

    b. Facing the possibility of supporting false teachers (v. 7-11)

3. The current recipients

C. The aim

1. To promote fellowship and joy based on love and truth (v. 1-3, 12-13)

2. To protect believers from being deceived and supporting false teachers (v. 4-11)

Detailed Outline of 2 John

Living out love, in truth.

I. **The Truth Promotes Love—The Truth Issues in Love, Especially for Other Believers (v. 1-3)**

    A. **John's love (v. 1-2)**

        1. The personal aspect of John's love [I love]

        2. The sphere of John's love [in truth]

        3. The source of John's love [v. 2, the indwelling Spirit of Truth]

    B. **All believers' love (v. 1-2)**

        1. The corporate identity of those who love [all who know the truth]

        2. The common source of their love [v. 2, the indwelling Spirit of Truth]

    C. **God's love (v. 3)**

        1. The gifts of God's love

            a. *Grace*

            b. *Mercy*

            c. *Peace*

        2. The assurance of God's love

        3. The source of God's love

        4. The inseparability of God's love from truth

II. Love promotes the truth (v. 4-11)

    A. Love rejoices in obedience to God's truth (v. 4)

    B. Love is realized in obedience to God's Word of truth (v. 5-8)

        1. The command to love (v. 5)

        2. The definition of love (v. 6)

        3. The reasons for love (v. 7-8)

            a. Deceivers deny salvation by denying the truth (v. 7)

            b. There is a full reward for faithfulness to the truth (v. 8)

    C. Love does not receive or support those who contradict the truth about Christ (v. 9-11)

        1. The truth about the doctrine of Christ (v. 9)

        2. The truth about supporting false teachers (v. 10-11)

            a. The command not to support (v. 10)

            b. The consequences of support (v. 11)

III. Love and truth promote fellowship and joy (v. 12-13)

    D. True fellowship desires more than merely written communication (v. 12)

    E. True fellowship produces fullness of joy (v. 12c)

    F. True fellowship is based on God's sovereign grace (v. 13)

3 John

Kress Biblical Resources

Overview Outline of 3 John

Living out the truth, in Love.

I.   Intro: Cultivate your love for people and the practice of the truth [holiness] (1-4)

　　A.   Love for people (which inevitably leads to prayer for them) (v. 1-3)

　　B.   Love for the practice of the truth [holiness/obedience to God's Word] (v. 4)

II. Continue on in faithful service of the brethren, love and support of the ministry (v. 5-8)

　　A.   Continue in faithful service (v. 5)

　　B.   Continue in love (v. 6a)

　　C.   Continue to support the ministry [missionary support] (v. 6b-8)

III. Contemplate the ways of the arrogant (v. 9-10)

　　A.   Self-promoting (v. 9a)

　　B.   Unteachable/unsubmissive/ultimately uncommitted to the Word of God (v. 9b)

　　C.   Reproachable (v. 10a)

　　D.   Slanderous/untrue and unwholesome words (v. 10b)

　　E.   Inhospitable/unloving (v. 10c)

　　F.   Overbearing leadership/dictatorial leadership (v. 10d)

IV. Commit yourself to imitate good – not evil (v. 11)

　　A.   Because it evidences the new birth (v. 11a)

　　B.   Because without it, it evidences spiritual blindness (v. 11b)

V.   Consider the testimony about the praiseworthy person (v. 12)

　　A.   All people in general acknowledge his character (v. 12a)

　　B.   The Word of God affirms his character (v. 12b)

　　C.   Faithful leadership affirms his character (v. 12c)

VI. Conclusion: Convey personal interest to those you minister to and with (v. 13-15)

A. Fellowship involves more than just written communication (v. 13)

B. Fellowship includes a desire for personal interaction (v. 14)

C. Fellowship includes prayer and affectionate regard for those in Christ (v. 15)

Introductory Matters

I. **Introduction**

   A. **The author**

      1. The human author

         a. *His designation (v. 1a)*

         b. *His authority (v. 4-5, 10-11)*

         c. *His literary similarities to 1, 2 John and the Gospel of John*

      2. The divine author (cf. 2 Tim. 3:16-17)

   B. **The audience**

      1. The original recipients

         a. *Gaius—a believer who faithfully supports the ministry (v. 1, 3, 5-6)*

         b. *Possibly facing the opposition of Diotrephes (v. 9-11)*

      3. The current recipients

   C. **The aim**

      1. To encourage Gaius in his faith (v. 1-4)

      2. To encourage Gaius to continue to support traveling ministers who are preaching the truth, even if they are strangers to him personally (v. 5-11)

      3. To promote fellowship in truth and love (v. 13-15)

Detailed Outline of 3 John

Living out the truth, in love.

I. **Intro: Cultivate your love for people and the practice of the truth [holiness] (1-4)**

   A. **Love for people (which inevitably leads to prayer for them) (v. 1-3)**

      1. A proclamation of love (v. 1)

      2. A prayer of love (v. 2)

      3. A praise for love lived out—in truth (v. 3)

   B. **Love for the practice of the truth [holiness/obedience to God's Word] (v. 4)**

II. **Continue on in faithful service of the brethren, love and support of the ministry (v. 5-8)**

   A. **Continue in faithful service (v. 5)**

      1. To believers who are known

      2. To believers who are strangers

   B. **Continue in love (v. 6a)**

   C. **Continue to support the ministry [missionary support] (v. 6b-8)**

      1. The manner of support (v. 6b)

      2. The motives for support (v. 7-8)

         a. *The like-minded goal [the glory of Christ] (v. 7a)*

         b. *The sincerity of the missionaries (v. 7b)*

         c. *The mandate from God to be co-laborers with Him (v. 8)*

III. Contemplate the ways of the arrogant (v. 9-10)

    A.　Self-promoting (v. 9a)

    B.　Unteachable/unsubmissive/ultimately uncommitted to the Word of God (v. 9b)

    C.　Reproachable (v. 10a)

    D.　Slanderous/untrue and unwholesome words (v. 10b)

    E.　Inhospitable/unloving (v. 10c)

    F.　Overbearing leadership/dictatorial leadership (v. 10d)

IV. Commit yourself to imitate good – not evil (v. 11)

    A.　Because it evidences the new birth (v. 11a)

    B.　Because without it, it evidences spiritual blindness (v. 11b)

V. Consider the testimony about the praiseworthy person (v. 12)

    A.　All people in general acknowledge his character (v. 12a)

    B.　The Word of God affirms his character (v. 12b)

    C.　Faithful leadership affirms his character (v. 12c)

VI. Conclusion: Convey personal interest to those you minister to and with (v. 13-15)

    D.　Fellowship involves more than just written communication (v. 13)

    E.　Fellowship includes a desire for personal interaction (v. 14)

    F.　Fellowship includes prayer and affectionate regard for those in Christ (v. 15)

Jude

Kress Biblical Resources

Overview Outline of Jude

Contending for the Faith

I. The epistolary introduction (v. 1-4)

A. The author (v. 1)

B. The audience (v. 2)

C. The appeal for God's mercy, peace and love (v. 3)

D. The aim (v. 3-4)

II. The examples of God's judgment upon the ungodly (v. 5-19)

A. The punishment of the ungodly illustrated (v. 5-10)

B. The pretense of the ungodly illustrated (v. 11-13)

C. The prophecy of Enoch concerning the ungodly (v. 14-16)

D. The prophecy of the Apostles concerning the ungodly (v. 17-19)

III. The exhortations to the godly in the midst of growing apostasy (v. 20-23)

A. Stay in the love of God (v. 20-21)

B. Show mercy to the doubting (v. 22)

C. Save some out of the fire (v. 23a)

D. Show mercy on those completely ensnared, but be careful not to be contaminated by their evil (v. 23b)

IV. The exclamation of praise to the Sustainer and Savior of His people (v. 24-25)

A. Praise Him for His power and protection (v. 24a)

B. Praise Him for His provision of grace, holiness, and joy (v. 24b)

C. Praise Him for His Person (v. 25)

<u>Introductory Matters</u>

I.   Introduction (v. 1-4)

A. The author

1.   The human author (v. 1a)

   a.   *His name*

   b.   *His calling*

   c.   *His brother*

2.   The divine author (cf. 2 Tim. 3:16-17)

B. The audience

1.   The original recipients (v. 1b, 3, 4, 5-11)

   a.   *Believers (v. 1b, 3)*

   b.   *Facing the infiltration of false teachers (v. 4)*

   b.   *Familiar with the Old Testament Scriptures (v. 5-11)*

3.   The current recipients

C. The aim

1.   To encourage believers concerning God's love and preservation (v. 1-2, 24-25)

2.   To exhort believers to remember (v. 5a, 17-18)

   a.   *Remember the Old Testament examples of God's dealings with the ungodly (v. 5-16)*

   b.   *Remember the Apostles' warnings concerning the coming of the ungodly (v. 17-28)*

3.   To exhort believers to contend for the faith in the face of false teachers who have infiltrated the church (v. 3-4)

Detailed Outline of Jude

Contending for the Faith

I.   **The epistolary introduction (v. 1-4)**

   A. **The author (v. 1a)**

   B. **The audience (v. 1b)**

   C. **The appeal for God's mercy, peace and love (v. 2)**

   D. **The aim (v. 3-4)**

   1.   The purpose of the epistle (v. 3)

   2.   The presence of ungodly among the church (v. 4)

II. **The examples of God's judgment upon the ungodly (v. 5-19)**

   A. **The punishment of the ungodly illustrated (v. 5-10)**

   1.   The selective examples (v. 5-7)

   a.   Those who did not believe in the Exodus generation (v. 5)

   b.   Those angels who did not keep their own domain (v. 6)

   c.   Those cities including Sodom and Gomorrah that pursued gross immorality (v. 7)

   2.   The similarities of the ungodly to these examples (v. 8-10)

   a.   They are dreamers who defile the flesh and reject authority (v. 8)

   b.   They do not have the proper respect for God's order (v. 9)

   c.   They live by their instincts like animals (v. 10)

   B. **The pretense of the ungodly illustrated (v. 11-13)**

   1.   The selective examples (v. 11)

   a.   The way of Cain—religion without faith

   b.   The error of Balaam—religion for profit

   c.   The rebellion of Korah—religion for power

2.   The sad illustrations of their deceptive character (v. 12-13)

    a.   Hidden reefs (v. 12a)

    b.   Clouds without water (v. 12b)

    c.   Autumn trees without fruit (v. 12c)

    d.   Wild waves of the sea (v. 13a)

    e.   Wandering stars (v. 13b)

C.   The prophecy of Enoch concerning the ungodly (v. 14-16)

1.   The antediluvian prophecy (v. 14-15)

    a.   The prophet Enoch (v. 14a)

    b.   The prophecy of the ungodly (v. 14b-15)

2.   The attributes of the ungodly (v. 16)

D.   The prophecy of the Apostles concerning the ungodly (v. 17-19)

1.   The prophecy of the Apostles (v. 17-18)

    a.   The modern era cited (v. 17)

    b.   The mockers predicted (v. 18)

2.   The problems attendant to the ungodly (v. 19)

III. The exhortations to the godly in the midst of growing apostasy (v. 20-23)

    A. Stay in the love of God (v. 20-21)

    B. Show mercy to the doubting (v. 22)

    C. Save some out of the fire (v. 23a)

    D. Show mercy on those completely ensnared, but be careful not to be contaminated by their evil (v. 23b)

IV. The exclamation of praise to the Sustainer and Savior of His people (v. 24-25)

    A. Praise Him for His power and protection (v. 24a)

    B. Praise Him for His provision of grace, holiness, and joy (v. 24b)

    C. Praise Him for His Person (v. 25)

        1. He is the only God

        2. He is Savior

            a. *Because of His character*

            b. *Because of the Person and Work of Jesus Christ*

        3. He is the eternal origin and object of all glory, majesty, dominion and authority

Revelation

KF

The Revelation

From and *About* *

JESUS CHRIST

to the beloved Apostle John

for the Church

THE BIG PICTURE

Part 1
The <u>Past</u> Preparatory *Vision* of the Prophet
(1:1-20)

Part 2
The <u>Present</u> Pictorial *Condition* of the People
(2:1-3:22)

Part 3
The <u>Future</u> Panoramic *Prediction* of the Prophet
(4:1-22:5)

---

*The *"Revelation"* is *"from"* Jesus Christ (1:1). "About" is included in this title to underscore the uncovered magnitude and splendor of our Lord Jesus Christ within His Revelation.

Special thanks to Dr. Timothy L. Dane, whose notes and discussions have helped me formulate this outline, and to Dr. George J. Zemek, a friend, mentor and guardian of the Word, who continues to pass the exegetical torch.

In my collection of works on the book of Revelation, one commentary stands out as the most exhaustive, helpful and scholarly of them all. It is the two-volume commentary by Dr. Robert L. Thomas: *Revelation 1-7 and Revelation 8-22, An Exegetical Commentary* (Chicago: Moody Press, 1992). Thank you Dr. Thomas for your clear, concise, and confirming comments.

PART 1

The <u>Past</u> Preparatory Vision of the Prophet *(1:1-20)*[1]

I. **The Prophet's <u>Prologue</u> for the Revelation *(1:1-8)***

    A. **The *Preface* of the Revelation Announced *(1:1-3)***

        1. The *<u>Title</u>* of the Revelation – *"The Revelation" (1:1a)*

        2. The *<u>Transmission</u>* of the Revelation – ***Generally (1:1b)***

            a. The *Source* – God Gives *(1:1b)*

            b. The *Stipulation* – Christ Shows *(1:1b)*

            c. The *Slaves* – Believers Receive *(1:1b)*

        3. The *<u>Things</u>* in the Revelation *(1:1c)*

            a. Things to Happen *Surely* – *"must" (1:1c)*

            b. Things to Happen *Shortly* – *"soon" (1:1c)*

        4. The *<u>Type</u>* of Revelation – Words and Symbols *(1:1d)*[2]

        5. The *<u>Transmitters</u>* of the Revelation *(1:1b, e, 2a)*

            a. God *Reveals (1:1b)*

            b. Jesus *Receives (1:1b)*

            c. The Angel *Reiterates* – *"communicated it by His angel" (1:1e)*[3]

            d. John *Writes (1:1e, 2a)*

---

[1] Things to note for the use of this outline: 1. All Scripture quotations are taken from the *New American Standard Bible* (Lockman Foundation, 2003). 2. The biblical texts quoted are *italicized* and appear in *"double quotes."* 3. Some points in the outline have more than one Scripture reference (e.g., 1:1a, c, 2a). 4. On occasion, the references to the biblical texts are <u>not</u> placed in chronological order. This is purposely done in order to organize certain themes and subjects within the outline. 5. This outline is intended to be used alongside of an open Bible.

[2] Though symbols are used throughout the Revelation, it is to be interpreted using the same literal, grammatical, historical, geographical and theological method used to interpret the rest of the Bible.

[3] The word *"communicated"* renders a verb in the Greek, which basically means *signified* (sign-i-fied). Cf. Rev. 1:2, *"all that he saw."*

6. The *Transmission* of the Revelation – *Specifically (1:2)*

    a. John's *Witness* for Jesus – *"testifies" (1:2a-b)*

        i. To the *Words* of God *(1:2a)*

        ii. To the *Witness* of Jesus *(1:2b)*

    b. John's *Eyewitness* for Jesus – *"all that he saw" (1:2c)*

7. The *Target* of the Revelation *(1:3)*

    a. The Blessed *Reader (1:3a)*

    b. The Blessed *Hearer (1:3b)*

    c. The Blessed *Heeder (1:3c)*

8. The *Timing* of the Revelation – *"time is near" (1:3d)*

B. The *People* Addressed in the Revelation *(1:4-5c)*

1. The *Author* – Servant John *(1:4a)*

2. The *Addressees* – Seven Churches *(1:4a)*

3. The *Appeal* – Sincere Greetings *(1:4b-5c)*

    a. The *Substance* of It Anticipated in the Greeting *(1:4b)*

        i. *Grace* for the Churches *(1:4b)*

        ii. *Peace* for the Churches *(1:4b)*

    b. The *Source* of It Announced in the Greeting *(1:4c-5c)*

        i. Grace and Peace from God the *Father (1:4c)*

        ii. Grace and Peace from God the *Spirit (1:4d)*[4]

        iii. Grace and Peace from God the *Son (1:5a-c)*

            (1) His *Surety* – *"faithful witness" (1:5a)*

            (2) His *Superiority* – *"firstborn of the dead" (1:5b)*

            (3) His *Sovereignty* – *"ruler of the kings" (1:5c)*

C. The *Praise* Ascribed in the Revelation *(1:5d-6)*

1. The *Direction* of the Doxology *(1:5d-6a)*

    a. To the Son Who *Prizes* Us – *"loves us" (1:5d)*

    b. To the Son Who *Pardoned* Us – *"released us" (1:5e)*

    c. To the Son Who *Promoted* Us – *"made us" (1:6a)*

---

[4] The *"Holy Spirit"* is represented by 7 *"spirits"* (Rev. 1:4; 3:1; cf. Isa. 11:1-2), 7 *"lamps of fire"* (Rev. 4:5), 7 *"horns"* and 7 *"eyes"* (Rev. 5:6), and 7 *"lampstands"* (Zech. 4:1-10). Also note the end of each letter to the 7 churches, where the Spirit speaks to each one (Rev. 2:7, 11, 17, 29; 3:6, 13, 21).

2. The *Devotion* of the Doxology *(1:6b)*

THE 1ˢᵀ PSALM: *Praise the Love of Christ*[5]

"To Him who loves us and released us from our sins by His blood – and He has made us to be a kingdom, priests to His God and Father – to Him be the glory and the dominion forever and ever. Amen."

     a.   For the Son's Perpetual *Splendor (1:6b)*

     b.   For the Son's Perpetual *Strength (1:6b)*

D. The *Premise* of the Revelation Asserted *(1:7-8)*

1. The *Vindication* of the Son *(1:7)*

     a.   In His *Cloud* Coming – *"with the clouds" (1:7a)*

     b.   In His *Clear* Coming – *"every eye will see Him" (1:7b)*

     c.   In His *Comprehensive* Coming – *"the tribes of the earth" (1:7c)*

     d.   In His *Convicting* Coming – *"mourn over Him" (1:7d)*

     e.   In His *Confirmed* Coming – *"So it is to be. Amen" (1:7e)*

2. The *Verification* of the Father *(1:8)*

     a.   By His *Immutability* – *"Alpha and Omega" (1:8a)*

     b.   By His *Eternality* – *"is and who was and who is to come" (1:8b)*

     c.   By His *Potency* – *"the Almighty" (1:8c)*[6]

II. The Prophet's <u>Preparation</u> for the Revelation *(1:9-20)*

A. The *Designation* of John – *"I John" (1:9a)*

B. The *Affliction* of John *(1:9)*

1. The *Partaker* in Our Affliction *(1:9a-b)*

     a.   Fellow Partaker in *Tribulation (1:9a)*

     b.   Fellow Partaker in The *Kingdom (1:9b)*

     c.   Fellow Partaker in *Jesus (1:9b)*

2. The *Place* of His Affliction – *"Patmos" (1:9c)*

---

[5] The theme of "worship" is often overlooked by many who study the Revelation. In addition to the intriguing visions of future events, glorious descriptions of Jesus Christ appear. There are times when the 4 *"living creatures,"* the 24 *"elders,"* *"an angel,"* *"angels,"* people and / or creatures break out in praise. The texts of 15 **Psalm-like** passages *(songs, doxologies, prayers* or *proclamations)* are included in this outline for emphasis on worship (4:8d; 4:11; 5:9-14; 7:10a; 7:12; 11:15; 11:17-18; 12:10-12; 15:3-4; 16:5-6, 7; 19:1-2; 19:6-8). The **Psalms** appear in ***Bold Italics***, e.g. ***"to Him be glory."***

[6] The title *"Almighty"* refers to the LORD's omnipotence.

3. The *Purpose* of His Affliction *(1:9d)*

     a. Because of the *Word* of God *(1:9d)*

     b. Because of the *Witness* of Jesus *(1:9d)*

C. The *Condition* of John *(1:10a)*

1. In the *"spirit" (1:10a)*[7]

2. On a *Sunday (1:10a)*

D. The *Commission* of John – *Generally (1:10b-11)*

1. The *Individual* Giving the Commission *(1:10b)*

     a. His Declaration – *"like the sound of a trumpet" (1:10b; cf. 4:1)*

     b. His Designations – *"first . . . last . . . living One," (cf. 1:17-18a)*

2. The *Instructions* Given in the Commission *(1:11)*

     a. *Pen* the Vision *(1:11a)*

     b. *Post* the Vision *(1:11b)*[8]

E. The *Vision* of Jesus *(1:12-16)*

1. Jesus *Encircled* by Seven Lampstands – The Churches *(1:12-13a; cf. 1:20)*[9]

2. Jesus *Exposed* as Son of Man – Messiah *(1:13b-16)*[10]

     a. His *Sonship* Title – *"a son of man" (1:13b)* [11]

     b. His *Stately* Clothing – Dignity *(1:13c)*

     c. His *Splendid* Girdle – Messenger *(1:13d)*

     d. His *Snow-like* Head – Wisdom *(1:14a)*

     e. His *Searing* Eyes – Omniscience *(1:14b)*

     f. His *Shining* Feet – Purity *(1:15a)*

     g. His *Sounding* Voice – Omnipotence *(1:15b)*

     h. His *Sword-like* Tongue – Victorious *(1:16b)*

     i. His *Sun-like* Appearance – Glory *(1:16c)*

3. Jesus *Embraced* Seven Stars *(1:16a, cf. 1:20)*

---

[7] Some translations have "Spirit." In light of the context, "spirit" is preferable (cf. 4:2; 17:3; 21:10). John was evidently transformed into some altered state, since his normal senses would be inadequate to see Christ and comprehend the incredible vision of the future (cf. 4:2; 17:3; 21:10).

[8] The Revelation was to be posted to the *"seven churches"* named in chapters 2 - 3.

[9] Rev. 1:20 interprets *"lampstands"* as *"the seven churches"* addressed in chapters 2 - 3.

[10] Notice the words *"like"* and *"as."* These likenesses may refer to attributes of Christ as John attempts to describe his heavenly vision of Jesus in earthly terms.

[11] See Daniel 10:5-6 for a similar description.

F. The *Trepidation* of John – *"like a dead man" (1:17a)*

G. The *Consolation* of Jesus *(1:17b-18)*

    1. The Comfort of Jesus' <u>Hand</u> – *"right hand on me" (1:17b)*

    2. The Command for John's <u>Heart</u> – *"Do not be afraid" (1:17b)*

    3. The Continuance and Confirmation of Jesus' <u>Help</u> *(1:17c-18)*

        a. Jesus, the *Eternal* One – *"the first and the last" (1:17c)*

        b. Jesus. the *Ever-abiding* One – *"the living One" (1:18a)*

        c. Jesus, the *Ever-present* One – *"alive forevermore" (1:18b)*

    4. The Control of Jesus over <u>Hades</u> *(1:18c)*

H. The *Commission* of John – *Specifically (1:19)*[12]

    1. Write the Past <u>Vision</u> – *"which you have seen" (1:19a)*

    2. Write the Present <u>Condition</u> – *"which are" (1:19b)*

    3. Write the Prophetic <u>Revelation</u> – *"which will take place" (1:19c)*

I. The *Interpretation* of John's Vision *(1:20, cf. 1:16)*

    1. Stars – <u>Messengers</u> *(1:20a; cf. 1:16a)*[13]

    2. Lampstands – <u>Churches</u> *(1:20b; cf. 1:12-13a)*

---

[12] Rev. 1:19 establishes 3 major parts of the book, which this outline follows: PART 1 – *"the things which you have seen,"* namely, the vision of Christ (Rev. 1:10-20), PART 2 – *"the things which are,"* particularly, the condition of the churches being addressed (2:1-3:22), and PART 3 – *"the things which will take place,"* obviously, the contents of the body of the book that reveal future events (Rev. 4:1-22:11). PART 4, mercifully includes an invitation from Jesus (Rev. 22:6-21).

[13] Some translate *angeloi* as "angels." It <u>may</u> be best translated as "messengers," referring to human representatives from each church who may have had leadership responsibilities.

PART 2

The <u>Present</u> Pictorial Condition of the People *(2:1-3:22)*[14]

I.   **The Message for <u>Elapsing Ephesus</u>** *(2:1-7)*

     A.   The *Designation* of the Church – *"Ephesus"* *(2:1a)*

     B.   The *Description* of Christ – 7 Stars, 7 Lampstands *(2:1b)*

     C.   The *Discernment* of Christ – *"I know…"* *(2:2a)*

     D.   The *Deeds* of the Church – Testing, Persevere *(2:2b-3, 6)*

     E.   The *Difficulty* within the Church – Left First Love *(2:4)*

     F.   The *Discipline* for the Church – Lamp Removed *(2:5b)*

     G.   The *Desire* of Christ – *"Remember," "Repent"* *(2:5a, c)*

     H.   The *Desire* of the Spirit – *"hear…overcomes"* *(2:7a)*

     I.   The *Destination* of the Overcomers – *"Paradise"* *(2:7b)*

II.   **The Message for <u>Suffering Smyrna</u>** *(2:8-11)*

     A.   The *Designation* of the Church – *"Smyrna"* *(2:8a)*

     B.   The *Description* of Christ – *"the first and last," "dead, and has come to life"* *(2:8b)*

     C.   The *Discernment* of Christ – *"I know…"* *(2:9a)*

     D.   The *Difficulty* within the Church – Trials, Poverty *(2:9b)*

     E.   The *Delusion* in the Church – *"synagogue of Satan"* *(2:9c)*

     F.   The *Desire* of Christ – *"Do not fear…be faithful"* *(2:10)*

     G.   The *Desire* of the Spirit – *"hear…overcomes"* *(2:11a)*

     H.   The *Delight* of the Overcomers – The *"crown of life,"* No *"second death"* *(2:10c, 11d)*

---

[14] See Diagram 1, *Seven Parallel Messages for Seven Prominent Churches.*

III.　**The Message for** <u>Perceiving Pergamum</u> *(2:12-17)*

　　A.　**The *Designation* of the Church** – *"Pergamum" (2:12a)*

　　B.　**The *Description* of Christ** – *"two-edged sword" (2:12b)*

　　C.　**The *Discernment* of Christ** – *"I know…" (2:13a)*

　　D.　**The *Difficulty* within the Church** – *"Satan's throne,"* *"where Satan dwells" (2:13b, d)*

　　E.　**The *Deeds* of the Church** – Faith, Martyrdom *(2:13c)*

　　F.　**The *Delusion* in the Church** – Holding to Errant Teachings, Immorality *(2:14-15)*

　　G.　**The *Desire* of Christ** – *"Repent" (2:16a)*

　　H.　**The *Discipline* for the Church** – *"the sword" (2:16b)*

　　I.　**The *Desire* of the Spirit** – *"hear…overcomes" (2:17a)*

　　J.　**The *Delicacy* and *Delight* of the Overcomers** – *"manna,"* *"stone," "new name" (2:17b)*

IV.　**The Message for** <u>Tolerating Thyatira</u> *(2:18-29)*

　　A.　**The *Designation* of the Church** – *"Thyatira" (2:18a)*

　　B.　**The *Description* of Christ** – *"Son of God,"* Fiery Eyes, Bronze Feet *(2:18b)*

　　C.　**The *Discernment* of Christ** – *"I know…" (2:19a)*

　　D.　**The *Deeds* of the Church** – *"love," "faith," "service,"* *"perseverance" (2:19b)*

　　E.　**The *Difficulty* within the Church** – *"Jezebel" (2:20-21)*

　　F.　**The *Discipline* for the Church** – Sickness, Death *(2:22-23)*

　　G.　**The *Disciples* in the Church** – *"the rest" (2:24)*

　　H.　**The *Desire* of Christ** – *"Hold fast" (2:25)*

　　I.　**The *Destination* of the Overcomers** – Rule with Christ, Receive *"morning star" (2:26-28)*

　　J.　**The *Desire* of the Spirit** – *"Hear" (2:29)*

V.   The Message for <u>Sleeping Sardis</u> *(3:1-6)*

    A.   The *Designation* of the Church – *"Sardis" (3:1a)*

    B.   The *Description* of Christ – 7 *"Spirits," 7 "stars" (3:1b)*[15]

    C.   The *Discernment* of Christ – *"I know…" (3:1c)*

    D.   The *Delusion* in the Church – *"dead" (3:1d)*

    E.   The *Desire* of Christ – *"Wake up," "strengthen," "remember," "repent" (3:2a, 3a)*

    F.   The *Discipline* for the Church – Surprise Visit *(3:3b)*

    G.   The *Disciples* in the Church – Worthy Walkers *(3:4)*

    H.   The *Delight* of the Overcomers – *"white garments," "book of life" (3:5)*

    I.   The *Desire* of the Spirit – *"Hear" (3:6)*

VI.   The Message for <u>Faithful Philadelphia</u> *(3:7-13)*

    A.   The *Designation* of the Church – *"Philadelphia" (3:7a)*

    B.   The *Description* of Christ – *"holy," "true" (3:7b)*

    C.   The *Discernment* of Christ – *"I know…" (3:8a)*

    D.   The *Deeds* of the Church – *"kept My word," "not denied My name" (3:8b)*

    E.   The *Destitute* in the Church – *"synagogue of Satan," (3:9)*

    F.   The *Disciples* in the Church – *"perseverance" (3:10a)*

    G.   The *Desire* of Christ – Kept *"from the hour of testing," "hold fast," "crown" (3:10b, 11)*

    H.   The *Destination* of the Overcomers – Pillar in God's Temple with His Name *(3:12)*

    I.   The *Desire* of the Spirit – *"Hear" (3:13)*

---

[15] For more on the 7 *"Spirits of God"* cf. Rev. 1:10; 4:5; 5:6, and see Footnote 4. For the 7 "stars," cf. Rev. 1:20. See Footnote 13.

VII. The Message for <u>Lukewarm Laodicea</u> *(3:14-22)*

A. The *Designation* of The Church – *"Laodicea" (3:14a)*

B. The *Description* of Christ – *"Amen," "Witness," "Beginning of the creation" (3:14b)*[16]

C. The *Discernment* of Christ – *"I know..." (3:15a)*

D. The *Destitute* in the Church – *"neither cold nor hot," "poor, blind and naked" (3:15b, 17)*

E. The *Discipline* for the Church – *"spit you out" (3:16, 19a)*

F. The *Desire* of Christ – Be Cold Or Hot, *"become rich," "repent,"* etc. *(3:15c, 18-20)*

G. The *Destination* of the Overcomers – On Throne *(3:21)*

H. The *Desire* of the Spirit – *"Hear" (3:22)*

The wonderful vision of the Lord Jesus Christ (1:10-20), and the weighty descriptions of Him in the opening of the letters to the churches (2:1-3:22), now give way to the prophecy portraying what the Lord will enact in the future. Prepare to witness waves of wrath on earth and waves of worship in heaven, which will take place in the waning days of world history.

---

[16] The meaning of the word *"beginning"* conveys the Greek sense of *source*. NASB's margin has, "I.e. Origin or Source."

PART 3

The <u>Future</u> Panoramic Prediction of the Prophet *(4:1-22:5)*[17]

I.   John's <u>Preparation</u> for the Prophecy *(4:1-5:14)*

   A.   John *Before the Throne* of God *(4:1-11)*

      1.   John's *Soar* to the Throne of God *(4:1-2a)*

         a.   The *Threshold* to Heaven – *"door standing open" (4:1a)*

         b.   The *Trumpet* from Heaven – *"voice . . . said, 'Come'" (4:1b)*[18]

         c.   The *Things* in Heaven – *"what must take place" (4:1c)*

         d.   The *Transport* to Heaven – *"in the spirit" (4:2a, cf. 1:10)*

      2.   The *Sovereign* on the Throne of God *(4:2b-3a)*

         a.   The Throne *Standing* – For Attention *(4:2b)*

         b.   The One *Sitting* – For Adoration *(4:2c)*

         c.   The One *Shining* – For Awe *(4:3a)*

      3.   The *Surroundings* of the Throne of God *(4:3b-8b)*

         a.   The *Sight* of It *(4:3b, 5a, 6a)*

            i.   The *Rainbow* around It *(4:3b)*

            ii.   The *Lightning* from It *(4:5a, 6a)*

            iii. The *Glass* before It *(4:6a)*

         b.   The *Servants* – 24 Elders around It *(4:4)*[19]

         c.   The *Sounds* – Thunder and Voices from It *(4:5a)*

         d.   The Holy *Spirit* – 7 Lamps of Fire before It *(4:5b)*[20]

         e.   The *Singers* – 4 Living Beings near It *(4:6b-8b)*[21]

---

[17] Chapters 4-5 are introductory and preparatory to the prophetic portion of the Revelation (6:1-22:5). John is transported to heaven from where the ordained events will proceed. He describes the scenes leading up to the commencement of the wrath of the Lamb and the wonders awaiting His people.

[18] The trumpet-like *"voice"* is most likely that of Christ (cf. 1:10).

[19] Some understand the 24 *"elders"* to be representatives of the Church. This outliner believes they are high ranking angels, lower than the 4 Living Beings. They seem to act, speak, and reveal like other angels throughout the Revelation. The 24, along with the 4, are distinct from the redeemed (5:9-10), and followed by *"myriads"* of angels (5:11).

[20] Cf. 1:4; 3:1; 5:6. See Footnote 4.

[21] *"Creatures"* may be better understood as "beings." Perhaps they are the highest order of angels, even above the Cherubim and Seraphim described in the Old Testament. There are quite a few features that the Living Beings, Cherubim, and Seraphim share, but there are also many differences.

        i.   Their *Eyes* – *"full of eyes" (4:6b; 8b)*

        ii.   Their *Faces (4:7)*

            (1) 1st Being – Like a *Lion (4:7a)*

            (2) 2nd Being – Like an *Ox (4:7b)*

            (3) 3rd Being – Like a *Man (4:7c)*

            (4) 4th Being – Like an *Eagle (4:7d)*

        iii. Their *Wings* – *"six" (4:8a)*

4.   The *Solemnity* Before the Throne of God *(4:8c-11)*

    a.   The *Reverence* of the 4 Living Beings *(4:8c-d)*

        i.   Their *Persistence* – No Rest *(4:8c)*

        ii.   Their *Praise (4:8d)*

           THE 2ND PSALM: *Praise the Eternal One*

           "Holy, holy, holy is the Lord God, the Almighty,

           Who was and who is and who is to come."

    b.   The *Response* of the 24 Elders *(4:9-11)*

        i.   *Following* the 4 Beings *(4:9)*

        ii.   *Falling* before God *(4:10a)*

        iii. *Worshipping* before God *(4:10b)*

        iv. *Casting* Crowns before God *(4:10c)*

        v.   *Praising* God *(4:11)*

           THE 3RD PSALM: *Praise the Creator*

           "Worthy are You, our Lord and our God,

           to receive glory and honor and power;

           for You created all things,

           and because of Your will they existed, and were created."

B. John *Before the Lamb* of God *(5:1-14)*

1.   The *Setting* – *At* God's Throne *(5:1a)*

2.   The *Scroll* – *In* God's Hand *(5:1b)*[22]

---

[22] There are many views as to what the *"book"* represents or contains (the Lamb's book of life, the title deed to the earth, the New Covenant, etc.). This outliner holds the view that the *"book"* (scroll) contains the final phase of God's redemptive plan, which is both wrath and salvation contained **in the Revelation**. The "sealed up" prophecy of Daniel (Dan. 12:4) is now opened and magnified. Jesus is worthy not only to open it for examination; He opens it for execution.

    a. *Secure* in God's Hand *(5:1b)*

    b. *Inscribed* by God's Hand *(5:1b)*

    c. *Sealed* for God's Plan *(5:1b)*

3.   The <u>*Suspense*</u> – *Around* God's Throne *(5:2-5)*

    a. The Strong *Angel's* Question – *"Who is worthy?" (5:2)*

    b. The Solemn *Heavenly* Answer – No one! *(5:3)*

    c. The *Apostle's* Sad Reaction – *"weep" (5:4)*

    d. The *Elder's* Salutary Answer – The Lamb Has Overcome! *(5:5)*

        i.   The *Lion of Judah* Prevails! *(5:5a)*

        ii.   The *Root of David* Prevails! *(5:5b)*

4.   The <u>*Savior*</u> – *In the Midst of* God's Throne *(5:6-8)*

    a. The Lamb's *Servants* – The 4/24 *(5:6)*[23]

        i.   The *4 Living Beings (5:6a)*

        ii.   The *24 Elders (5:6b)*

    b. The Lamb *Standing* – His Prominence *(5:6c)*

    c. The Lamb *Slain* – His Redemption *(5:6c)*

    d. The Lamb's *Spirit* – His 7 *"horns,"* 7 *"eyes" (5:6d)*[24]

    e. The Lamb's *Supremacy* – *"He took the book." (5:7)*

    f. The Lamb's *Servants* – The 4/24 *(5:8)*

        i.   The 4/24 *Falling* before the Lamb *(5:8a)*

        ii.   The 4/24 *Holding* the Prayers of the Saints *(5:8b)*

5.   The <u>*Song*</u> – *To* God and the Lamb *(5:9-14)*

THE 4TH PSALM: *Praise the Lamb*

    a. 1st Stanza – The Heavenly *Singers* – The 4/24 *(5:9-10)*

    Worthy Is the Redeemer

    "Worthy are You to take the book and to break its seals;

    for You were slain, and purchased for God with Your blood

    men from every tribe and tongue and people and nation.[25]

    You have made them to be a kingdom and priests to our God;

    and they will reign upon the earth."

---

[23] *The 4/24* stands for the 4 Living Beings and the 24 *"elders"* when mentioned together in the Revelation.

[24] Cf. 1:4; 3:1; 4:5. See Footnote 4.

[25] These 4 terms (*tribe, tongue, people,* and *nation*), referring to representatives of every people group, appear 5 times in the Revelation (5:9; 7:9; 11:9; 13:7; 14:6).

    b. 2nd Stanza – More Heavenly *Singers* – Myriads *(5:11-12)*

      Worthy Is the Lamb

      "Worthy is the Lamb that was slain to receive power and riches and wisdom and might and honor and glory and blessing."

    c. 3rd Stanza – Even More Heavenly *Singers* – All Creatures *(5:13)*

      Worthy Is the Father and the Son

      "To Him who sits on the throne, and to the Lamb, be blessing and honor and glory and dominion forever and ever."

    d. Encore *(5:14)*

      i. The 4 Living Beings Say, *"Amen" (5:14a)*

      ii. The 24 Elders *"fell down and worshiped" (5:14b)*

II. John's <u>Presentation</u> of the Prophecy *(6:1-22:5)*[26]

A. The LAMB Initiates 6 Seals for *Punishment* – The Wrath *(6:1-17)*

1. The 4 *Horsemen* – It's Only Just Begun! *(6:1-8)*[27]

    a. **1st Seal** – *Pseudo Peace (6:1-2)*

      i. The *Call* of the 1st Living Being – *"Come"* To See *(6:1)*

      ii. The *Color* of the Horse – *"white" (6:2a)*

      iii. The *Character* of the Rider – An Exploiter *(6:2b-d)*

        (1) *Wielding* a Bow *(6:2b)*

        (2) *Wearing* a Crown *(6:2c)*

        (3) *Waging* to Conquer *(6:2d)*

    b. **2nd Seal** – *World War (6:3-4)*

      i. The *Call* of the 2nd Living Being – *"Come"* To See *(6:3)*

      ii. The *Color* of the Horse – *"red" (6:4a)*

      iii. The *Character* of the Rider – An Executioner *(6:4b-d)*

---

[26] See Diagram 2, *Ordering Revelation's Chapters.* Chapter 6 begins the prophetic section of the Revelation. The events from 6:1-19:21 take place during Daniel's 70th Week, i.e., *The Tribulation, Jacob's Trouble.*

[27] The riders of these horses are not to be taken as literal individuals. They are images of types of judgments imposed upon the earth by God. These waves of wrath come upon mankind in the form of external damage (death and destruction) as well as internal deception (cf. 2 Thess. 2:11, *"God will send upon them a deluding influence..."*).

        (1) *Taking* Peace *(6:4b)*

        (2) *Killing* People *(6:4c)*

        (3) *Swinging* Sword *(6:4d)*

  c. **3rd Seal** – *Famine and Fortune (6:5-6)*

     i. The *Call* of the 3rd Living Being – *"Come"* To See *(6:5a)*

     ii. The *Color* of the Horse – *"black" (6:5b)*

     iii. The *Character* of the Rider – An Extortioner *(6:5c-6)*

        (1) *Carrying* a Scale *(6:5c)*

        (2) *Causing* a Starvation *(6:6a-b)*[28]

        (3) *Creating* a Shortage *(6:6c)*

  d. **4th Seal** – *Death and Darkness (6:7-8)*

     i. The *Call* of the 4th Living Being – *"Come"* To See *(6:7)*

     ii. The *Color* of the Horse – *"ashen" (6:8a)*

     iii. The *Character* of the Rider – An Extinguisher *(6:8b-d)*

        (1) Named *"Death" (6:8b)*

        (2) Followed by *"Hades" (6:8c)*

        (3) Caused Death – (sword, hunger, beasts, etc.) *(6:8d)*

2. **The 2 _Heralds_ *(6:9-17)* Who can stand, the martyrs or the wicked?**

  a. **5th Seal** – *Massive Martyrdom* – **Revenge!** *(6:9-11)*

     i. The *Cause* of Their Martyrdom *(6:9)*

        (1) Slain for the *Word of God (6:9a)*

        (2) Slain for their *Witness of Jesus (6:9b)*

     ii. The *Cry* of the Martyrs – *"How long?" (6:10)*

        THE 5TH PSALM: *A Prayer for Deliverance*

        "How long, O Lord, holy and true, will You refrain from judging and avenging our blood on those who dwell on the earth?"

     iii. The *Color* of Their Robes – *"white" (6:11a)*

     iv. The *Character* of Their Interval *(6:9a, 11b)*

        (1) Their *Residence* – Under the Altar *(6:9a)*

        (2) Their *"Rest"* – Until Others Join *(6:11b)*

---

[28] Notice the *"voice"* from the midst of the 4 Living Beings; it is probably the voice of the Lamb. Cf. Rev. 1:10; 4:1.

b. **6ᵗʰ Seal** – *Withering Wicked* – **Relinquish!** *(6:12-17)*

   i. The *Immediate Case* for Their Withering *(6:12-14b)*

     (1) Brutal *Earthquake* (*6:12a*)

     (2) Blackened *Sun (6:12b)*

     (3) Blood *Moon (6:12c)*

     (4) Blistering *Meteors (6:13)*

     (5) Buckling *Skies (6:14a)*

     (6) Breaking *Mountains* and *Islands (6:14b)*

   ii. The *Inevitable Complaint* in Their Withering *(6:15-16a)*

     (1) Their *Character* – Kings, Mighty, Slave, Free *(6:15a)*

     (2) Their *Cover* – Rocks and Caves *(6:15b)*

     (3) Their *Cry* – *"Fall on us" (6:16a)*

   iii. The *Intentional Cause* of Their Withering *(6:16b-17)*

     (1) The *Display* of Wrath – *"wrath of the Lamb" (6:16b)*

     (2) The *Day* of Wrath – *"great day of their wrath" (6:17)*

B. The LAMB Intervenes for *Protection* – The Witnesses *(7:1-17)*

1. The Messengers of Israel *Protected (7:1-8)*

a. The Angels' *Control* of the *Natural Elements (7:1-3)*

   i. The 4 Angels *Preparing* Harm for the Masses *(7:1)*

     (1) Standing at the *4 Corners* of the Earth *(7:1a)*

     (2) Holding Back the *4 Winds* of the Earth *(7:1b)*

   ii. The 1 Angel *Preventing* Harm of the Messengers *(7:2-3)*

     (1) *Coming* From the East *(7:2a)*

     (2) *Clutching* the Seal *(7:2b)*

     (3) *Commanding* the 4 Angels *(7:2c-3)*

       (a) His *Cry* – *"Do not harm" (7:2c-3a)*

       (b) His *Condition* – *"until we seal" (7:3b)*

b. The Lord's *Commission* of the *National Elect (7:4-8; cf. 14:1-5)*

   i. Their *Number* – 144,000 *(7:4)*

   ii. Their *Names (7:5-8)*[29]

---

[29] Judah is mentioned first, probably due to it being the tribe of the Messiah. There are 19 lists of the 12 tribes; they contain different names in various orders, causing much debate. For an interesting discussion regarding the inclusion of *"Levi"* and *"Joseph"* and the

(1)   12,000 from *Judah (7:5a)*

(2)   12,000 from *Reuben (7:5b)*

(3)   12,000 from *Gad (7:5c)*

(4)   12,000 from *Asher (7:6a)*

(5)   12,000 from *Naphtali (7:6b)*

(6)   12,000 from *Manasseh (7:6c)*

(7)   12,000 from *Simeon (7:7a)*

(8)   12,000 from *Levi (7:7b)*

(9)   12,000 from *Issachar (7:7c)*

(10) 12,000 from *Zebulun (7:8a)*

(11) 12,000 from *Joseph (7:8b)*

(12) 12,000 from *Benjamin (7:8c)*

2.   The Multitude of Saints *Perfected (7:9-17)*

    a.   The *Description* of the Multitude *(7:9-17)*

       i.   Their *Population* – From Everywhere *(7:9a-b)*

          (1)   Their *Number* – *"no one could count" (7:9a)*

          (2)   Their *Nature (7:9b, cf. 5:9)*

             (a) Of *Nations (7:9b)*

             (b) Of *Tribes (7:9b)*

             (c) Of *Peoples (7:9b)*

             (d) Of *Tongues (7:9b)*

       ii.   Their *Position* – *Before* God and the Lamb *(7:9c, 15a-b)*

          (1)   Standing Before the *Throne* of God *(7:9c, 15a)*

          (2)   Standing Before the *Lamb* of God *(7:9c)*

          (3)   Serving in the *Temple* of God *(7:15b)*

       iii.   Their *Perfection* – *Based On* the Lamb's Blood *(7:9d, 10b, 13, 14b)*

          (1)   *Clothed* by Christ *(7:9d, 13)*

          (2)   *Saved* by God *(7:10b)*

          (3)   *Washed* by the Lamb *(7:14b)*

---

absence of *Dan* and *Ephraim* in this list, see Dr. Robert L. Thomas, *Revelation 1-7, An Exegetical Commentary* (Chicago: Moody Press, 1992), pages 478-482.

       iv. Their *Preservation – From* the Lamb's Wrath *(7:14a, 10a, 15b)*

          (1) Saved *Out of* the Tribulation *(7:14a)*

          (2) Saved *to* Worship and Serve *(7:10a, 15b)*

       v. Their *Protection – In* God and the Lamb *(7:9c, 15c)*

          (1) Present with the *Lamb (7:9c)*

          (2) Present with *God (7:15c)*

      vi. Their *Provisions – By* God and the Lamb *(7:16-17)*

          (1) No More *Starving (7:16a)*

          (2) No More *Thirsting (7:16a)*

          (3) No More *Sweating (7:16b)*

          (4) No More *Wandering (7:17a)*

          (5) No More *Crying (7:17b; cf. 21:4)*

  b. The *Devotion* of the Multitude *(7:9d, 10b, 15b)*

       i. Their *Worship* of the Lamb – With Palm Branches *(7:9d)*

      ii. Their *Worship* of God *(7:10b)*

      THE 6ᵀᴴ PSALM: *Praise the Deliverer*

      "Salvation to our God who sits on the throne,
      and to the Lamb."

      iii. Their *Service* to God and the Lamb *(7:15b)*

  c. The *Devotion* of Heaven *(7:11-12)*[30]

       i. Their *Description* – The 4/24 and Angels *(7:11)*

      ii. Their *Doxology (7:12)*

      THE 7ᵀᴴ PSALM: *Sevenfold Praise to God*

      "Amen, blessing and glory and wisdom
      and thanksgiving and honor
      and power and might,
      be to our God forever and ever. Amen."

---

[30] In some cases, as here, the Scripture references are rearranged for the sake of organizing the content into an outline. See Footnote 1.

C. The LAMB Initiates *More Punishment (8:1-9:21)*
The 7ᵗʰ Seal Containing 7 Trumpets

1. *Silence* in Heaven – **Get Ready!** *(8:1-3)*

   a. *Shhhh* for ½ Hour *(8:1)*

   b. *Seven Angels* Stand before God *(8:2a)*

   c. *Seven Trumpets* for Seven Angels *(8:2b)*

   d. *Saints'* Prayers before God – **"Justice!"** *(8:3)*

2. *Storms* on Earth *(8:4-6)*

   a. Incense *Prayers Go Up* to God *(8:4)*

   b. Intervening *Punishment Goes Down* to Earth *(8:5)*

   c. Inevitable *Preparation* for Sounding the Trumpets *(8:6)*

3. *Sounds* of the First 4 Trumpets *(8:7-12)*

   a. **1ˢᵗ Trumpet** – *Fiery Hail (8:7)*

      i. The *Wrath* – Bloody Hail and Fire *(8:7a)*

      ii. The *Result (8:7b-d)*

         (1) 1/3 of the Earth Burned *(8:7b)*

         (2) 1/3 of the Trees Burned *(8:7c)*

         (3) All of the Grass Burned *(8:7d)*

   b. **2ⁿᵈ Trumpet** – *Fiery Mountain (8:8-9)*

      i. The *Wrath* – A Burning Mountain *(8:8a)*

      ii. The *Result (8:8b-9)*

         (1) 1/3 of the *Salt Water* Polluted *(8:8b)*

         (2) 1/3 of the *Sea Creatures* Died *(8:9a)*

         (3) 1/3 of the *Ships* Destroyed *(8:9b)*

   c. **3ʳᵈ Trumpet** – *Fiery Star (8:10-11)*

      i. The *Wrath* – A Burning Comet *(8:10)*

      ii. The *Result (8:11)*

         (1) 1/3 of the Fresh Water Polluted *(8:11a)*

         (2) Death from the *"Wormwood"* Waters *(8:11b)*

   d. **4ᵗʰ Trumpet** – *Fading Skies (8:12)*

      i. The *Wrath* – Celestial Bodies Struck *(8:12a)*

      ii. The *Result* – 1/3 of the Light Snuffed *(8:12b)*

4. *Severe "**Woes**"* from Midheaven *(8:13-9:21)*

    You ain't seen nothing yet!

    a. The Angelic *Announcement* of the **3 Woes** –
        The Last 3 Trumpets *(8:13)*[31]

    b. **1st Woe – 5th Trumpet** – *Locust* Demons *Excruciate (9:1-11)*

        i. The *Appointment* of the Demons – By a Fallen Star *(9:1a)*

        ii. The *Abode* of the Demons – From the Pit *(9:1b-2)*

        iii. The *Ascension* of the Demons – To the Earth *(9:3)*

        iv. The *Activity* of the Demons – To Sting *(9:4-5a)*

        v. The *Agony* from the Demons – To Torment *(9:5b-6, 10b)*

        vi. The *Appearance* of the Demons – *"Like" (9:7-10a)*[32]

            (1) Horses – *Powerful (9:7a)*

            (2) Crowns – *Victorious (9:7b)*

            (3) Man's Face – *Intelligent (9:7c)*

            (4) Woman's Hair – *Seductive (9:8a)*

            (5) Lion's Teeth – *Fierce (9:8b)*

            (6) Breastplates – *Protected (9:9a)*

            (7) Wings – *Swift (9:9b)*

            (8) Scorpion Tails – *Tormented (9:10)*

        vii. The *Authority* Over the Demons *(9:11)*

            (1) The *Origination* of the Leader – *"the abyss" (9:11a)*

            (2) The *Designation* of the Leader *(9:11b-c)*

                (a) Hebrew – *Abaddon* = Destroyer *(9:11b)*

                (b) Greek – *Apollyon* = Destroyer *(9:11c)*

    c. **One *"woe"* down; two *"woes"* to go!** *(9:12)*

---

[31] The 7th *"seal"* contains the 7 *"trumpets."* The last 3 *"trumpets"* are preceded by the angelic announcement, *"Woe, Woe, Woe."* This outliner refers to them as, the "Woe Trumpet" (9:1), the "Woe, Woe Trumpet" (9:13), and the "Woe, Woe, Woe Trumpet" (16:2), which contains the 7 *"bowls."*

[32] Notice the words *"like"* and *"as."* These likenesses <u>may</u> refer to characteristics of the demons as John attempts to describe his heavenly vision of the future in earthly terms.

d. **2ⁿᵈ Woe – 6ᵗʰ Trumpet** – *Lots of* Demons *Exterminate (9:13-19)*

   i. The *Appointment* of the Demon Armies *(9:13-14)* [33]

     (1) Released *by* the Lamb *(9:13-14a)* [34]

     (2) Released *from* the Euphrates *(9:14b)*

   ii. The *Angels* over the Demon Armies *(9:15)*

     (1) 4 Prepared for the *Divine Time (9:15a)*

     (2) 4 Prepared for the *Divine Torment (9:15b)*

   iii. The *Amount* of the Demon Armies – 200,000,000 *(9:16)*

   iv. The *Appearance* of the Demon Armies *(9:17, 19)*

     (1) Horse-like *Bodies (9:17a)*

     (2) Fiery *Breastplates (9:17b)*

     (3) Lion-like *Heads (9:17c)*

     (4) Flaming *Mouths (9:17d, 19a; cf. 18b)*

     (5) Serpent-like *Tails (9:19b)*

   v. The *Atrocity* of the Demon Armies – 1/3 Killed *(9:18)*

e. **Still, mankind does not repent!** [35] *(9:20-21)* [36]

---

[33] Some view these armies as human armies. Others conclude that John is describing an army of demons. In favor of demon armies (probably leading human armies) is the use of *"like,"* which is also used to describe the *"locust"* demons in the previous paragraph (9:1-11).

[34] Notice the *"voice from the four horns of the golden altar which is before God."* This may be the voice of Jesus Christ Himself.

[35] Four times it is stated that the earth-dwellers *"did not repent,"* even after enduring the heavy outpouring of the Lamb's wrath (Rev. 9:20, 21; 16:9, 11).

[36] The *mostly* chronological deployment of the Lamb's wrath will pick up again at 15:1, after a **pause** for inspiration and information contained in chapters 10-14. See Diagram 2, *Ordering Revelation's Chapters.*

D. PAUSE for *Inspiration*! 7th trumpet is just ahead! *(10:1-11:18)* [37]

1. Bitter Sweet <u>*Wrath*</u> in the Revelation *(10:1-11)*

   a. The Voice of Another *Mighty Angel (10:1-7)*

      i. His *Description* – The Wonder *(10:1)*

         (1) Formidable *Figure (10:1a)*

         (2) Cloudy *Clothes (10:1b)*

         (3) Colorful *Crown (10:1c)*

         (4) Flaming *Face (10:1d)*

         (5) Fiery *Feet (10:1e)*

      ii. His *Possession* – The Word *(10:2a)*[38]

      iii. His *Position* – The World *(10:2b, 5a)*

      iv. The *Reverberation* – The War Cries *(10:3)*

         (1) First, the Angel's Lion-like Voice *(10:3a)*

         (2) Second, the Lord's Thunder-like Voice *(10:3b; 4a)*[39]

      v. His *Petition* – The Wait *(10:4b-c)*

         (1) Seal Up! *(10:4b)*

         (2) Write Not! *(10:4c)*

      vi. His *Declaration* – The Wrath *(10:5-7)*

         (1) The Angel's *Vow (10:5-6)*

            (a) His *Posture* – *"right hand to heaven" (10:5)*

            (b) His *Pledge (10:6)*

               (i) The Solemn *Oath* – Sworn by God *(10:6a-b)*

               (ii) The Sure *Outcome* – No Delay! *(10:6c)*

---

[37] Chapters 10-14 form a break in the *mostly* chronological Revelation. In 3 ways, this section forms a **pause** for John and future readers. First, to **encourage** John and believers who are confronted with the awful days in store for the saints and the world. Second, to **equip** us with important details concerning events within the judgment period (*Daniel's 70th Week, 7-Year Tribulation, Jacob's Trouble;* more specifically the *3 ½ years; 42 months; 1230 days; time, time and half a time*). Third, to **endow** us with significant background for the coming 7 *"bowl"* judgments contained in the 7th *"trumpet."* Other **pauses** are for <u>reflection</u> (Rev. 16:5-7), <u>motivation</u> (Rev. 16:15), and <u>specification</u> (Rev. 17-18).

[38] Though the *"little book"* contains awful judgements, its inspiration comes from the knowledge that God's wrath comes upon a deserving, sinful world.

[39] The angel's lion-like voice is different from the voice of the 7 *"thunders."* Most likely, the thunder-like *"voices"* are / is God's confirmation of the terror in the *"little book."*

(2) The Lord's *Vengeance* – **It is finished!** *(10:7)*[40]

   (a) The *"Mystery" Completed* in the Future *(10:7a)*

   (b) The *"Mystery" Conveyed* in the Past *(10:7b)*

b. The Voice from *Heaven* – Take the book! *(10:8; cf. 10:3b)*[41]

c. The Voice of the *Mighty Angel* – Eat the book! *(10:9)*

   i. *Sour* in the Tummy *(10:9a)*

   ii. *Sweet* on the Tongue *(10:9b)*

d. The Voice of *John (10:10)*

   i. *Sweet* on the Tongue – Yeah, Get 'em God! *(10:10a)*

   ii. *Sour* in the Tummy – Oh, God Got 'em. *(10:10b)*

e. The Voice of the *Mighty Angel* – *"prophesy again" (10:11)*[42]

2. **Bold Speaking *Witnesses* in the Tribulation *(11:1-13)*[43]**

a. Their *Prophecy (11:1-3)*

   i. The *Topography* – Concerning Jerusalem *(11:1-2a)*

   ii. The *Trouble* – Conveying Genuine Grief *(11:2b, 3b)*

   iii. The *Time* – Consisting of 42 Mos. / 1260 Days *(11:2b, 3b)*

   iv. The *Type* – Containing God's Power *(11:3a)*

b. Their *Portrayal (11:4)*[44]

   i. Two Standing *Olive Trees (11:4a)*

   ii. Two Standing *Lampstands (11:4b)*

c. Their *Power (11:5-6)*

   i. Power to Protect *Prophesying (11:5)*

   ii. Power to Regulate *Rain (11:6a)*

   iii. Power to Redden *Rivers (11:6b)*

   iv. Power to Produce *Pandemics (11:6c)*

---

[40] The *"little book"* contains the *"mystery of God"* made up of the events associated with the Tribulation and the 1000-Year Kingdom spoken of by the Old Testament prophets. The details of the salvation and glorification of the saints and their eternal state are made clear by further information found in the New Testament, specifically in this Revelation.

[41] Probably the voice of God (or Christ) who *"thundered"* in verse 3.

[42] The prophecy John is to *"write"* continues at 11:1, ending at 22:5, completing the Revelation John received in the *"little book."* Chapters 11-14 are part of the **pause** of 10-14, and contain specific details of events to take place during the Tribulation. The chronology of the 7 *"seals"* and 6 *"trumpets"* left off at 9:21 and will pick up again at 15:1 with the sounding of the 7th *"trumpet."*

[43] While including the events associated within the Tribulation, more inspiration comes in knowing that God's 2 *"witnesses"* will be victorious.

[44] See Zech. 4:1-10.

    d. Their *Persecution (11:7-10)*

        i. *Slaughtered* by the *"Beast"* – After 3 ½ Years *(11:7)*[45]

        ii. *Sullied* in the Streets – Jerusalem *(11:8)*

        iii. *Slandered* by the World – For 3 ½ Days *(11:9-10)*

            (1) Their *Bodies* Positioned for View *(11:9)*

            (2) Their *Enemies'* Perceived Victory *(11:10)*

    e. Their *Preservation (11:11-13)*

        i. *Raised* by the LORD *(11:11)*

        ii. *Raptured* into Heaven *(11:12)*

        iii. *Regretted* by Their Enemies *(11:13)*

            (1) 1/10 Jerusalem *Destroyed (11:13a)*

            (2) 7,000 Jerusalemites *Died (11:13b)*

            (3) The Rest *Dismayed (11:13c)*

3. **Don't forget, two *"woes"* down; one *"woe"* to go. *(11:14)***

4. Blessed Sounds of *Worship* in Heaven *(11:15-18)*

    a. The *7ᵗʰ Trumpet* Sounds *(11:15a)*

    b. The *Heavenly Voices* Sound *(11:15; cf. Psa. 2)*

    THE 8ᵀᴴ PSALM: *Thy Kingdom Has Come*

    "The kingdom of the world has become

    the kingdom of our Lord and of His Christ;

    and He will reign forever and ever."

    c. The *Elders'* Voices Sound *(11:16-18)*

        i. Their *Posture* – *"fell on their faces" (11:16)*

        ii. Their *Praise (11:17-18)*

        THE 9ᵀᴴ PSALM: *A Song of Thanksgiving*

            (1) 1ˢᵗ Stanza *(11:17)*

            Devotion to the Almighty

            "We give You thanks, O Lord God, the Almighty,

            who are and who were, because You have taken

            Your great power and have begun to reign."

---

[45] The *"beast"* is the Antichrist. He is the 2ⁿᵈ *"Beast"* referred to in 13:2-8, who comes out of the *"abyss"* (13:1; 17:8). See also Footnote 48. For the time of their prophesying, cf. 11:2b and 3b. Also see Diagram 3, *The 7/8 Mountains.*

(2) 2nd Stanza *(11:18)*

    Devastation of the Angry

    "And the nations were enraged,

    and Your wrath came,

    and the time came for the dead to be judged,

    and the time to reward

    Your bond-servants the prophets

    and the saints and those who fear Your name,

    the small and the great,

    and to destroy those who destroy the earth."

E. Remain PAUSED for Additional *Information* – Still Awaiting the 7th Trumpet *(11:19-14:20)*[46]

1. *Displays* <u>from</u> Heaven *(11:19; cf. 16:17-21)*[47]

    a. The *Temple* of God Unveiled – *"heaven opened" (11:19a)*

    b. The *Tempest* of God Unleashed – Lightning, Thunder, Earthquake, Hail *(11:19b)*

2. *Details* <u>Before</u> the 7th Trumpet *(12:1-14:18)*

    a. Three *Histories of Israel (12:1-13)*

        i. The 1st History – *Signs* of the Past – Satan's Hatred of Israel *(12:1-4b)*

            (1) 1st *Sign (12:1-2)*

                (a) The *Woman* – Israel *(12:1)*

                (b) The *Child* – Jesus *(12:2)*

---

[46] 11:19-14:20 is a continuation of the **pause** begun at 10:1 and contains additional information regarding events occurring during the Tribulation. See Footnote 42.

[47] See 4:5; 8:5; 15:5-8 and 16:17-21 for similar language depicting the anticipation of those in heaven and God's readiness to act. Revelation 11:19 and 16:17-21 form bookends for a major section describing events of the latter portion of the 7-Year Tribulation, specifically the last *"trumpet"* containing the 7 *"bowls."*

(2)   2nd *Sign (12:3-4b)*

    (a)   The *Dragon* – Satan *(12:3)*[48]

        (i)   Fiery Red *(12:3a)*

        (ii)   7 Heads and 10 Horns *(12:3b)*

        (iii) 7 Diadems *(12:3c)*

    (b)   The *Stars* – Demons *(12:4a-b)*

        (i)   Drawn *from* Heaven *(12:4a)*

        (ii)   Thrown *to* Earth *(12:4b)*

ii.   The 2nd History – A *Symbol* for the Present – Messiah in John's Day *(12:4b-5)*

    (1)   The Devil's *Intention (12:4b-c)*

        (a)   To *Destroy* Israel *(12:4c)*

        (b)   To *Devour* the Messiah *(12:4d)*

    (2)   The Savior's *Incarnation* – His Birth *(12:5a)*

    (3)   The Savior's *Exaltation* – His Ascent *(12:5b)*

iii.   The 3rd History – *Significance* for the Future – Israel in the Tribulation *(12:6-17)*

    (1)   The *Woman* on Earth *(12:6)*

        (a)   Her *Place* of Protection – Wilderness *(12:6a)*

        (b)   Her *Period* of Protection – 1260 Days *(12:6b)*[49]

    (2)   The *War* in Heaven *(12:7-9)*

        (a)   The *Contestants (12:7)* [50]

           (i)   *Michael* and His Angels *(12:7a)*

           (ii)   *Satan* and His Demons *(12:7b)*

        (b)   The *Consequences (12:8-9)*

           (i)   The Demons *Conquered* by Angels *(12:8)*

           (ii)   The Dragon *Cast* to Earth *(12:9a)*

           (iii) The Demons *Cast* to Earth, Again *(12:9b)*

---

[48] The *"dragon"* (Satan; 12:3), and the 1st *"beast"* (the world's dominant Empire; 13:1-2), also referred to as the *"scarlet beast"* (the Empire's composition and leader; cf. 17:3, 8-11), each have 7 *"heads"* and 10 *"horns."* The 2nd *"Beast"* (the Antichrist) is the leader of the dominant world Empire empowered by the *"dragon."* All 3 work together.

[49] *"1260 days"* (cf. Rev. 11:3; 12:6) is 3 ½ years, which refer to the last half of the 7-Year Tribulation (Dan. 9:27). Other designations for the same period of time are: *"42 months"* (Rev. 11:2; 13:5) and *"time, time and half a time"* (Dan. 7:25; 12:7; Rev. 12:14).

[50] See Dan. 12:1.

(3) The *Worship* in Heaven *(12:10-12)*

    THE 10TH PSALM: *A Song of Victory*

    (a) 1st Stanza – *The Lord's Salvation (12:10)*

        "Now the salvation, and the power,

        and the kingdom of our God

        and the authority of His Christ have come,

        for the accuser of our brethren

        has been thrown down,

        he who accuses them

        before our God day and night."

    (b) 2nd Stanza – *The People's Redemption (12:11)*

        "And they overcame him

        because of the blood of the Lamb

        and because of the word of their testimony,

        and they did not love their life

        even when faced with death."

    (c) 3rd Stanza – *The Devil's Ejection (12:12)*

        "For this reason, rejoice,

        O heavens and you who dwell in them.

        Woe to the earth and the sea,

        because the devil has come down to you,

        having great wrath,

        knowing that he has only a short time."

(4) The *War* on Earth *(12:13-17)*

    (a) The Dragon's Persecution of Israel *Amplified (12:13)*

    (b) The Lord's Protection of Israel *Specified (12:14)*

        (i) *Place* of Protection – *"wilderness" (12:14a)*

        (ii) *Period* of Protection – 3 ½ Years *(12:14b)*

    (c) The Dragon's Persecution of Israel *Intensified (12:15)*

    (d) The Dragon's Persecution of Israel *Nullified (12:16)*

    (e) The Dragon's Pursuit of God's People *Multiplied (12:17)*

    b. Three *Horrible Beasts* on Earth in the Tribulation *(13:1-18)*[51]

    Three blind beasts, see how they run!

        i. The **1ˢᵗ BEAST** – Last Days' *World Empire (13:1-2)*

          (1) His / Its *Portrayal (13:1-2a)*

            (a) Its *Emergence* – From the Sea *(13:1a)*[52]

            (b) Its *Empire(s)* – 7 Heads & 10 Horns *(13:1b)*[53]

            (c) It *Emblems* – 10 Blasphemous Diadems *(13:1c)*

            (d) It *Embodiment* – Leopard, Bear, Lion *(13:2a)*[54]

          (2) His / Its *Power* – From the *"Dragon" (13:2b)*

        ii. The **2ⁿᵈ BEAST** – Last Days' *World Ruler (13:3-4)*[55]

          (1) His *Power (13:3-4)*

            (a) *Raised* from Fatal Wound *(13:3; cf. 17:8)*[56]

            (b) *Rules* with Dragon's Authority *(13:4a)*

            (c) *Revered* by Earth Dwellers *(13:4b)*[57]

---

[51] Chapter 13, verses 1-2, depict the **1ˢᵗ beast** as the last days' dominant world Empire made up of 10 *"horns"* (kings / kingdoms). See Dan. 2:41-43; 7:23-24; cf. Rev. 17:8-18. Verses 3-8 designate the **2ⁿᵈ Beast** (the Antichrist) as its leader (Dan. 7:24b-26; 11:26-45; Matt. 24:15; 2 Thess. 2:4-5). Verses 11-17 distinguish the **3ʳᵈ Beast** (the False Prophet) as the promoter of the 2ⁿᵈ *"Beast"* during the Tribulation. Chapter 13 introduces two main characters (the Antichrist and False Prophet) in the Tribulation. Chapters 17-18 illustrate two main characteristics of a wicked religious / commercial system (*"Babylon," "the harlot"*) that seems to cooperate with, and possibly rival the Empire of the Antichrist at some point in the Tribulation. Chapter 19 reports the rout of all 3 *"beasts"* (Empire, Antichrist, and False Prophet) at the return of Christ. See Diagram 2, *Ordering Revelation's Chapters.*

[52] See 11:7 and 17:8, which say that the *"beast"* ascends from the *"abyss."*

[53] The *"dragon,"* and the 1ˢᵗ *"Beast,"* (also referred to as the *"scarlet beast"* in 17:3), both have 7 *"heads"* and 10 *"horns."* The "dragon" empowers the 'beast." See Footnote 48; cf. 12:3-4.

[54] See Daniel 7 where Greece is a *"leopard,"* Persia is a *"bear"* and Rome is a *"lion."* This final dominant world Empire will sport cruel and wicked features of all of the previous world Empires combined, making it exceedingly gruesome.

[55] Verses 1-2 seem to describe the last days' dominant world Empire, while verses 3-8 designate its leader. *"I saw one* (the 2ⁿᵈ *"Beast"* – Antichrist) *of his* (the 1ˢᵗ *"beast"* – Empire) *heads as if it had been slain."* In some cases, both the Empire and its leader are referred to as *"beast"* (Dan. 7:7-11; Rev. 13:1-8; 17:3, 8-14). In 17:8, the reference pertains to the Antichrist (2ⁿᵈ *"Beast"*) who *"was, is not, and is about to come out of the abyss."*

[56] Cf. Rev. 11:7; 17:8. See Footnote 75.

[57] *"Those who dwell on the earth"* is a phrase often used to refer to the wicked unbelieving world.

(2) His *Profanity (13:5-8a)*

    (a) The *Time* of It – 42 Months *(13:5)*

    (b) The *Target* of It – God And His People *(13:6)*

    (c) The *Type* of It *(13:7-8a)*

        (i) Causing *Saints* to Run from Him *(13:7a)*

        (ii) Causing *Sinners* to Worship Him *(13:7b-8a)*

iii. ENCOURAGEMENT & EXHORTATION *(13:8b-10)*[58]

(1) Preservation in the *Book of Life (13:8b; cf. 21:27)*

(2) Preservation in the *Midst of Persecution (13:9-10)*

    (a) Listen *Prudently (13:9)*

    (b) Endure *Patiently (13:10)*

iv. The **3rd BEAST** – Last Days' *World Prophet (13:11-18)*

(1) His *Portrayal (13:11)*

    (a) *Surfaces* from the Land *(13:11a)*

    (b) *Split* Tongue *(13:11b)*

    (c) *Sheep* Horns *(13:11b)*

(2) His *Purpose (13:12-15)*

    (a) To *Promote* the Beast – Antichrist *(13:12-13)*

        (i) *Despotism* from the *"Beast" (13:12a)*

        (ii) *Demand* to Worship the *"Beast" (13:12b)*

        (iii)*Deception* Through Satanic Signs *(13:13)*

    (b) To *Perform* His Own Deceiving Signs *(13:14a)*

    (c) To *Produce* the Beast's Image *(13:14b-15)*

        (i) *Commands* It to Be Built *(13:14b)*

        (ii) *Causes* It to Live *(13:14b-15a)*

        (iii)*Constructs* It to Be Worshipped *(13:15b)*

    (d) To *Propagate* the Beast's Insignia *(13:16-18)*

        (i) The *Mandate* – Right Hand or Forehead *(13:16)*

        (ii) The *Market* – No Commerce Without It *(13:17)*

        (iii)The *Mark* – The Number of a Man *(13:18)*

---

[58] Cf. 14:12. Two times, in two separate sections describing intense situations (Rev. 13:8-10; 14:12), believers are exhorted to endure persecution and reminded of their preservation in the *"book of life of the Lamb."*

   c. Two *Heavenly Scenes* at the End of the Tribulation *(14:1-5)*

      i. The 1st Scene – The *Victory* on Earth *(14:1)*

         (1) The LAMB's *Position* – Mt. Zion *(14:1a)*

         (2) The LAMB's *Participants (14:1b-c, 3b)*

            (a) The *Number* – 144,000 *(14:1b, 3b)*

            (b) The *Name* – His Name / Father's Name *(14:1c)*

      ii. The 2nd Scene – The *Voice* in Heaven *(14:2-5)*

         (1) The Angelic *Singers* of the *"New Song" (14:2)*

            (a) Their *Voices* – Like a Waterfall *(14:2a)*

            (b) Their *Instruments* – Harps *(14:2b)*

            (c) Their *Stage* – Before God's Throne *(14:2b)*

         (2) The Adjacent *Spectators* of the *"New Song" (14:3a)*[59]

         (3) The Astute *Students* of the *"New Song" (14:1b, 3b-5)*

            (a) Their *Quantity* – 144,000 *(14:1b, 3b)*

            (b) Their *Quality (14:4-5)*

               (i) *Purity* for the Lamb *(14:4a, 5)*

               (ii) *Pursuit* of the Lamb *(14:4b)*

               (iii) *Perfection* by the Lamb *(14:3c, 4c)*

               (iv) *Position* with the Lamb *(14:3d)*

   d. Four *Heavenly Heralds* above the Tribulation *(14:6-13)*

      i. The 1st Herald – The *Eternal Gospel*
of God *(14:6-7)*

         (1) *Another Angelic Messenger* from God *(14:6a)*

         (2) The *Audible Message* from the Angel *(14:6b-7)*

            (a) The *Recipients* – The World: Nations, Tribes, Tongues and Peoples *(14:6b)*

            (b) The *Request* – The Warning *(14:7)*

               (i) *Repent!* – Fear and Glorify God! *(14:7a)*

               (ii) *Reverence!* – Worship the Creator: Heaven, Earth, Sea and Waters *(14:7c)*

            (c) The *Reason* – **Final Wrath Has Come!** *(14:7b)*

---

[59] The angels sing the *"new song,"* but its content is not stated. However, the 144,000 are able to *"learn"* it.

    ii. The 2nd Herald – The *Eventual Fall*
of Babylon *(14:8-13)*

      (1) *Another Angelic Messenger* of God *(14:8a)*

      (2) The *Audible Message* from the Angel *(14:8b-c)*

        (a) Babylon's *Doom (14:8b)*[60]

        (b) Babylon's *Deceit (14:8c)*

   iii. The 3rd Herald – The *Everlasting Torment*
of the Beast Worshippers *(14:9-11)*

      (1) *Another Angelic Messenger* of God *(14:9a)*

      (2) *Audible* Message from the Angel *(14:9b, 11)*

        (a) Earth's *Recipients (14:9b, 11)*

        (b) Heaven's *Revenge (14:10-11)*

          (i) The *Passion* of God's Wrath *(14:10a)*

          (ii) The *Power* in God's Wrath *(14:10b, c)*

          (iii)The *Place* of God's Wrath *(14:10d)*

          (iv)The *Perpetuity* of God's Wrath *(14:11)*

  iv. ENCOURAGEMENT & EXHORTATION *(14:12)*[61]

      (1) Endure *Patiently (14:12a)*

      (2) Live *Faithfully (14:12b)*

   v. The 4th Herald – The *Everlasting Bliss*
of the Redeemed *(14:13)*

      (1) The *Voice* of the LAMB *(14:13a)*

      (2) The *Victory* of the Martyrs *(14:13b)*

      (3) The *Verification* of the Spirit *(14:13c)*

      (4) The *Vindication* of the Martyrs *(14:13d)*

 e. Two *Heavenly Harvests* from the Tribulation *(14:14-20)*

   i. The 1st Judgment Harvest – *The Cutting (14:14-16)*

      (1) The *Coming* Reaper– *"son of man" (14:14)*

        (a) Sitting on a *"white cloud" (14:14a)*

        (b) Wearing a *"golden crown" (14:14b)*

        (c) Holding a *"sharp sickle" (14:14c)*

---

[60] See chapters 17-18 for more information concerning the nature of and destruction of *"Babylon."*

[61] Cf. Rev. 13:8b-10. Also see Footnote 58.

(2) The *Command* to Reap – *"another angel" (14:15)*

    (a) The Hour Is *Right (14:15a)*

    (b) The Harvest Is *Ripe (14:15b)*

(3) The *Certain* Reaping – *"son of man" (14:16)*

ii. The 2nd Judgment Harvest – *The Crushing (14:17-20)*

    (1) The *Coming* Grape Gatherer – Yet, *"another angel" (14:17)*

    (2) The *Command* to Gather Grapes – Still, *"another angel" (14:18)*[62]

        (a) The Angel's *Position* – From the Altar *(14:18a)*

        (b) The Angel's *Power* – Over Fire *(14:18a)*

        (c) The Angel's *Petition* – To 1st Angel *(14:18b-c)*

           (i) The Sickle Is *Ready (14:18b)*

           (ii) The Grapes Are *Ripe (14:18c)*

    (3) The Certain *Gathering* of the Grapes *(14:19)*

    (4) The Certain *Crushing* of the Grapes *(14:20)*

        (a) The Geographical *Setting* – Israel *(14:20a)*

        (b) The Gruesome *Scene* – Bloody *(14:20b)*

F. *THE WRATH OF GOD IS DONE! (15:1-18:24)*[63]

The 3rd *"woe"* is the 7th *"trumpet."*

1. *PREPARATION* FOR GOD'S FINAL WRATH

Get Ready! *(15:1-8)*

a. The *Sign* in Heaven *(15:1)*

    i. 7 Angels with 7 *"plagues" (15:1)*

    ii. 7 Bowls with *"wrath" (15:1)*

b. The *Singing* in Heaven *(15:2-4)*

    i. The *Victorious* Saints – On *"something like a sea of glass" (15:2; cf. 4:6; 20:4)*

    ii. The *Victory* Song – *"of Moses and the Lamb" (15:3-4)*[64]

---

[62] Angels of various ranks appear in all but one chapter in the Revelation (13).

[63] Following the **pause** of chapters 10-14, the events anticipated since 9:21 are finally coming to pass. See Diagram 2 for the arrangement of chapters in Revelation.

[64] See the *Song of Moses* in Exodus 15:1-18 for parallel praises. To the celebration of the deliverance from Egypt is added praise for the greater deliverance from sin and all of Israel's enemies through the Passover Lamb – Jesus Christ.

THE 11TH PSALM: *Praise to the King*

"Great and marvelous are Your works,

O Lord God, the Almighty;

Righteous and true are Your ways, King of the nations!

Who will not fear, O Lord, and glorify Your name?

For You alone are holy;

For all the nations will come and worship before You,

For Your righteous acts have been revealed."

    c. The *Scene* in Heaven *(15:5-8)*

        i. The *Holy* Tabernacle – The Ark *(15:5)*

        ii. The *Heavenly* Angels *(15:6-7)*

           (1) Their 7 *Bowls* *(15:6a, 7)*

               (a) *Furnished* by the 4th Living Being *(15:6a, 7a)*

               (b) *Full* of God's Wrath *(15:6a, 7b)*

           (2) Their Bright *Apparel* *(15:6b)*

        iii. The *Holy* Temple – The Temple Itself *(15:8; cf. 15:5)*

           (1) *Filled* with God's Glory and Power *(15:8a)*

           (2) *Forbidden* Until Plagues Are Finished *(15:8b)*

2. *POURING OUT* OF GOD'S FINAL WRATH *(16:1-21)*

    a. The Commanding *Voice* of God – **Pour out the wrath!** *(16:1)*

    b. The Condemning *Vengeance* of God *(16:2-17a)*

        i. **1st Bowl** – GANGRENOUS RASH *(16:2)*[65]

        ii. **2nd Bowl** – GLOBAL RED TIDE *(16:3)*

        iii. **3rd Bowl** – GORY RIVERS *(16:4)*

        iv. **PAUSE** FOR REFLECTION – **They deserve it!** *(16:5-7)*

           (1) The Song of the Angel over the Waters *(16:5-6)*

THE 12TH PSALM: *Praise to the Judge*

"Righteous are You, who are and who were,

O Holy One, because You judged these things;

for they poured out the blood of saints and prophets,

and You have given them blood to drink.

They deserve it."

---

[65] The outline titles given to the bowl judgments are in BOLD in to highlight the intensity and rapid succession of the LAMB's final outpouring of wrath at the end of the Tribulation.

    (2) The Song of the Angel at the Altar *(16:7)*

       THE 13TH PSALM: *Praise to the Almighty*

       "Yes, O Lord God, the Almighty, True and righteous are Your judgments."

  v. **4th Bowl** – GLOBAL WARMING *(16:8-9a)*

  vi. **STILL, THEY WILL NOT REPENT!** *(16:9b)*

  vii. **5th Bowl** – GRAVE DARKNESS *(16:10a)*

  viii.**STILL, STILL, NO REPENTANCE!** *(16:10b-11)*

  ix. **6th Bowl** – GLOBAL WAR *(16:12-16)*

    (1) The *Path* Arranged – From the East *(16:12)*

    (2) The *People* Assembled *(16:13-14)*

      (a) The Gathering by *Frog Demons* – From Satan, Antichrist and False Prophet *(16:13)*

      (b) The Gathering of *Foreign Dignitaries* – From All Nations *(16:14a)*

    (3) **PAUSE** FOR MOTIVATION *(16:15)*

      (a) Jesus Is *Coming!* *(16:15a)*

      (b) Blessing for the Faithful *Watcher* *(16:15b)*

      (c) Blessing for the Faithful *Walker* *(16:15c)*

      (d) Jesus Is *Watching!* *(16:15d)*

    (4) The *Place – "Armageddon" (16:14b, 16)*[66]

  x. **7th Bowl** – GASPING FOR AIR *(16:17a)*

    Gone with the wrath!

c. The Concluding *Verdict* of God – **IT IS DONE!** *(16:17b-21)*

  i. The *Finality* of It *(16:17b)*

  ii. The *Fierceness* of It *(16:18-21a)*

    (1) *Crushing* Sounds *(16:18a)*

    (2) *Crushing* Shakes *(16:18b)*

    (3) Jerusalem *Divided (16:19a)*

    (4) Babylon *Destroyed (16:19b)*

    (5) *Fleeing* Mountains *(16:20)*

    (6) *Falling* Hailstones *(16:21a)*

d. **STILL, STILL, STILL, THEY DON'T REPENT!** *(16:21b)*

---

[66] Cf. Rev. 19:11-19. See Diagram 4 for *War of Armageddon.*

G. PAUSE For *Specification* –

"Babylon" and the Dominant World Empire *(17:1-18:24)*[67]

1. Judgment on Babylon's Spiritual *Harlotry* – Her Corrupting Charm *(17:1-18)*[68]

    a. Her *Introduction (17:1a-b, 3a)*

        i.   *By* an Angel *(17:1a)*

        ii. *In* the spirit *(17:3a, cf. 1:10; 4:2; 21:10)*

        iii. *By* Nature – *"harlot" (17:1b)*

        iv. *In* the Wilderness *(17:3a)*

    b. Her *Illustration (17:1c, 2, 3b-c, 4, 6a)*

        i.   *Sitting* on Many Waters – Influencing the Nations *(17:1c)*

        ii. *Seducing* All the Nations *(17:2, 4, 6a)*

            (1) Defined as *Licentious* – *"immorality" (17:2, cf. 1a)*

            (2) Described as *Luring (17:4)*

                (a) *Wearing* Purple and Scarlet *(17:4a)*

                (b) *Adorning* Gold and Precious Stones *(17:4b)*

                (c) *Holding* a Seductive Cup *(17:4c)*

            (3) Depicted as *Lethal* – *"blood of the saints" (17:6a)*

        iii. *Saddled* on a *"Scarlet Beast"* – Dominant World Empire Led by the 2nd *"Beast" (17:3b-c)*[69]

            (1) Its / His Blasphemous *Names (17:3b)*[70]

            (2) Its / His 7 *Heads* and 10 *Horns (17:3c)*[71]

---

[67] Chapters 17-18 function as another **"pause"** following the 7th *"bowl"* (Rev. 16:17-21) and preceding the victory of the Lamb at His coming (Rev. 19).

[68] John describes specific elements of the spiritual and economic character of Babylon (i.e. *"the woman,"* and *"the harlot"*) during the reign of the *"beast"*(s) in the Tribulation. The 1st *"beast"* (the dominant Empire made up of 10 *"horns"*) and its leader, the 2nd *"Beast"* (the Antichrist) along with the 3rd *"Beast"* (the False Prophet) are introduced in Chapter 13. Here, the *"harlot"* (*"woman," "Babylon"*) is distinct from the Beast(s)'s Empire.

[69] In chapter 17, the *"scarlet beast"* is the organized system (make-up, composition) of a dominant world Empire (10 *"horns"* = 10 Kings or Kingdoms) and especially its leader. The interpretation of the *"scarlet beast"* is given in verses 8-14.

[70] The dominant world Empire (1st *"beast"*) and its leader (2nd *"Beast," "scarlet beast"* / the Antichrist) are *"full of blasphemies."* For almost verbatim descriptions of the Antichrist, see Dan. 7:8, 25; 11:36; 2 Thess. 2:4 and Rev. 13:1, 5.

[71] See Diagram 3, *The 7/8 Mountains,* showing the 2nd *"Beast"* (Antichrist) and 10 *"horns"* coming against the *"harlot"* / *"Babylon"* after what seems to be a mutual partnership to gain ascendency (cf. 17:16-17). The *"woman"* (*"harlot"*), a seducing

c. Her *Insignia (17:5)*

     i. *"Mystery" (17:5a)*

     ii. *"BABYLON THE GREAT" (17:5b)*[72]

     iii. *"MOTHER OF ALL HARLOTS" (17:5c)*

d. The *Importance (17:6b-7)*

     i. John's *Astonishment* – Why? *(17:6b)*

     ii. The Angel's *Answer* – *"I will tell you the mystery" (17:7)*

e. The *Interpretation* – The Competing Evil Powers *(17:8-18)*

     i. In This Corner, Evil #1 – The *"woman" / "harlot" /*
        "Babylon" (17:1-7, 15-18)[73]

     ii. In That Corner, Evil #2 – The *"beast" / "scarlet beast"*
        (17:8-14)[74]

        (1) Its *Sovereignty* – The Empire (1st Beast) and Its Leader
           (2nd Beast) *(17:8; cf. 13:1-8)*

           (a) Its / His *Resuscitation* – *"was, is not, and is about*
              to come up" (17:8a, 11-17)[75]

           (b) Its / His *Origination (17:8b-c; cf. 11:7)*

              (i) From the *"abyss" (17:8b)*

              (ii) From the *"mountains" (cf. 17:9-11)*

           (c) Its / His *Destination* – *"destruction" (17:8b)*

        (2) Its *Symbolism* – The World Empire(s) *(17:9-11)*

---

murderous organized system becomes the object of the *"Beast's"* hatred following their cooperation (*"of one mind"*).

[72] *"Babylon"* has long stood for rebellion against God during all previous Empires (Gen. 10:9-10; 11:1-9; Jer. 51:7; Hab. 2:15-16), but more so here, with the final, vilest and most violent system to ever exist. For other descriptions of spiritual harlotry, see Nah. 3:1, 4; Isa. 23:15; Jer.3:8-9.

[73] A specific identification of the *"woman"* (*"harlot" / "Babylon"*) is not given at this point, since similar metaphors and symbols used elsewhere in Scripture are clear portrayals of false religion, idolatry and spiritual apostasy (i.e. *fornication, adultery, cup of abomination, Babylon*). See also Revelation 17:15-18:24 for more details of the character of this particular last days' *Babylon-like influence*, both religiously and economically.

[74] Remember, the *"harlot" / "woman" / "Babylon"*) is <u>distinct</u> from Beast(s)'s Empire (i.e. *"the scarlet beast"*) upon which the *"harlot"* rides. See Footnote 68.

[75] In 13:3, the world will be *"amazed"* when the Antichrist is healed of his *"fatal wound."* Here, in 17:8, he *"is about come up out of the abyss,"* causing people to *"wonder."* He will be the resurrected Satan-indwelt leader of the 7th *"head" / "mountain"* (a future *Rome-like* Empire).

(a) Its *Past* Characters – 7 Mountains *"are"* 7 World Empires *(17:9-10b)*[76]

    (i) The 5 *Fallen* Empires – Egypt, Assyria, Babylon, Greece, Persia *(17:9-10a)*

    (ii) The 1 *Current* Empire – Rome – *"one is"* *(17:10b)*

(b) Its 1 *Future* Empire's Character *(17:10c-11)*

    (i) Its Certainty – *"when he/it* (Rome-like) *comes"* *(17:10c)*

    (ii) Its Brevity – *"remain a little while."* *(17:10d)*

    (iii) Its Complexity – *"an eighth* (Rome-like's leader) *and is one of the seven"* *(17:11)*[77]

(3) Its *Sub-Kings* – 10 Horns *"are"* 10 Kings *(17:12-14)*

(a) Their *Authorization* – To Empower the *"Beast"* *(17:12-13)*

    (i) The *Shared* Rule – *"with the Beast"* *(17:12a)*

    (ii) Their *Short* Rule – *"for one hour"* *(17:12b)*

    (iii) Their *Surrendered* Rule – *"give their power and authority to the beast"* *(17:13)*

(b) Their *Determination* – To War Against the Lamb *(17:14a)*

(c) Their *Destruction (17:14b-e)*

    (i) Overcome by the *Lord Himself (17:14b-d)*

        1. His *Depiction* – *"Lamb"* *(17:14b)*

        2. His *Description* – *"Lord of lords"* *(17:14c)*

        3. His *Designation* – *"King of kings"* *(17:14d)*

---

[76] Chapter 13 views 7 world Empires (7 *"heads"*) as existing at the same time. Here in 17:9-10, the metaphor changes from *"heads"* to *"mountains."* The 7 world Empires are now viewed as successive kingdoms.

[77] The 7th *"head"* / *"mountain"* represents the future *Rome-like* Empire in the Tribulation. The leader of the 7th *Rome-like* Empire is called the *"eighth,"* but he is really *"one of the seven."* His power and control will dominate to the point that he, in and of himself, is an Empire. See Diagram 3, *The 7/8 Mountains,* for details of 17:8-11.

(ii) Overcome by the *Lamb's Armies (17:14e)*

    1. His *Called (17:14e)*

    2. His *Chosen (17:14e)*

    3. His *Faithful (17:14e)*

iii. Its *Struggle* – Internal Conflict *(17:15-18)*[78]

    (1) The Characters *(17:15, 16a, 18)*

        (a) The *"Waters"* – The Nations *(17:15, cf. 17:1b)*

        (b) The *"10 Horns"* – 10 Kings / Kingdoms *(17:16a)*

        (c) The 2nd *"Beast"* – The Antichrist *(17:16a)*

        (d) The *"Woman"* – A Capital City *(17:18)*[79]

    (2) The Conspiracy *(17:16-17)*

        (a) Their *Plan* – To *Establish* Their Dominion *(17:16)*

            (i) The *"Beast"* And 10 *Despise* the Woman / Harlot / Babylon *(17:16a)*

            (ii) The *"Beast"* And 10 *Devour* the Woman / Harlot / Babylon *(17:16b)*

        (b) God's *Plan* – To *Accomplish* His Decree *(17:17)*[80]

            (i) In His *Way* – *"God has put it in their hearts." (17:17a)*

            (ii) In His *Timing* – *"until the words of God will be fulfilled" (17:17b)*[81]

  2. Judgment On Babylon's <u>*Sensual*</u> Hunger – Her Commercial City *(18:1-24)*[82]

---

[78] The *"harlot"* (*"Mystery Babylon"*) will draw mankind into her own perverse religious system (chapter 17) and her own corrupt political materialistic society (chapter 18), **while** riding on (coexisting with, cooperating with, possibly controlling and definitely seducing) the Empire of the Antichrist, **for a while**.

[79] The *"woman"* (*"Babylon"*) <u>seems</u> to point to a literal capital-like *"city"* of a rival to the Antichrist and his dominant Empire. Some believe it may occupy the actual ancient ruins of Babylon. It <u>may be</u> a religious capital (<u>maybe</u> a *Rome-like* or *Mecca-like* city) and a political / commercial capital (<u>maybe</u> a *New York-like* or *Dubai-like* city), **possibly** in the same location in the Middle East, **not necessarily** at the site of ancient Babylon. See Diagram 3, *The 7/8 Mountains,* for more details related to *"Babylon"* and a capital *"city."*

[80] God **caused** the Antichrist and his 10 sub-kings to use the *"harlot"* / *"Babylon"* to gain dominance / prominence (*"of one mind"*), then to *"hate"* her afterward.

[81] **If** *"Babylon"* (the *"harlot,"* *"woman"*) includes her geographical location (or region), this <u>may</u> refer to the conflict between the *"king of the North"* (the *"beast"*) and the *"king of the South"* (the *"harlot"* / *"woman"* / *"Babylon"*) mentioned in Daniel 11:40.

a. The *Announcement* of Babylon's Fall *(18:1-3)*

    i. The *Bearer* of the Message – *"another angel" (18:1)*

    ii. The *Brunt* of the Message – *"fallen is Babylon" (18:2)*

    iii. The *Basis* of the Message – *"her immorality" (18:3)*

b. The *Annihilation* of Babylon *(18:4-8)*

    i. *Escape* Her Plagues! *(18:4)*

    ii. *Expect* Her Punishment! *(18:5-7)*

        (1) God *Remembers*! *(18:5)*

        (2) God *Renders*! *(18:6)*

        (3) Her *Pleasure* – Luxury *(18:7a)*

        (4) Her *Pride* – *"I sit as a queen." (18:7b)*

    iii. *Extinguished* as Her Punishment *(18:8)*

        (1) The *Moment* – In 1 Day *(18:8a)*

        (2) The *Manner* – Plagues, Death, Famine, Fire *(18:8b)*

        (3) The *Motive* – The Lord's Justice *(18:8c)*

c. The <u>*Agony*</u> of Babylon's Fall *(18:9-19)*[83]

    i. The Mourning of *Monarchs (18:9-10)*

        (1) The *Sound* from Its Burning – Weeping *(18:9a)*

        (2) The *Sight* of Its Burning – Smoking *(18:9b)*

        (3) The *Swiftness* of Its Burning – *"in one hour" (18:10)*

    ii. The Mourning of *Merchants (18:11-17a)*

        (1) Their *List* of Merchandise *(18:11-13)*

        (2) Their *Luxuries* Missed *(18:14)*

        (3) Their *Loss* as Merchants *(18:15a)*

        (4) Their *Lament* and Misery *(18:15b, 16a)*

        (5) Their *Loss* in a Moment – *"in one hour" (18:17a)*

    iii. The Mourning of *Mariners (18:17b-19)*

        (1) The *Sight* of Its Burning – Smoking *(18:17b)*

---

[82] There is a focus on the destruction of a *"strong city."* The city (*"Babylon"*) also stands for a religious, political, and commercial system that rides on the back of the Antichrist and his 10 horned Empire. They are allies, for a while.

[83] *"Babylon"* in chapter 18 <u>may</u> refer to a capital city of last days, which the Antichrist and the 10 *"horns"* will come against. The destruction of the *"Babylon"* (*"the harlot"* / *"woman"* / *"mystery Babylon"*) will come at the hands of the 2nd *"Beast"* and his 10 *"horns,"* which is an **ordained** internal struggle (Rev. 17:16-17; cf. Footnotes 70 and 72). Cf. Rev. 14:8; 17:3. See Diagram 3, *The 7/8 Mountains.*

    (2) The *Sound* of Its Burning – Weeping *(18:18-19a)*

    (3) The *Swiftness* of Its Burning – *"in one hour" (18:19b)*

  d. The *Applause* of Heaven *(18:20)*

    i. The *Voice* of Heaven *(18:20a)*

    ii. The *Vindication* of the Prophets *(18:20b)*

    iii. The *Vengeance* of God Himself *(18:20c)*

  e. The *Angel's* Final Blow *(18:21-24)*

    i. His *Example* – A Millstone *(18:21)*

    ii. Its *Extinction (18:22-23c)*

      (1) No More *Musicians (18:22a)*

      (2) No More *Mills (18:22b)*

      (3) No More *Majesty (18:23a)*

      (4) No More *Marriages (18:23b)*

      (5) No More *Merchants (18:23c)*

    iii. The *Explanation (18:23d-24)*

      (1) Because of Her *Magic (18:23d)*

      (2) Because of Her *Murders (18:24)*

H. THE *VICTORY* OF THE LAMB *(19:1-22:5)*

1. THE LORD GOD OMNIPOTENT *REIGNS (19:1-10)*[84]

  a. The *Music* of Victory *(19:1-8)*

    i. The *Angelic* Praise *(19:1-5)*

    THE 14TH PSALM: *The Hallelujah Chorus*

    (1) 1st Stanza – *Hallelujah, the Sound of Victory (19:1-2)*

      "Hallelujah!

      Salvation and glory and power belong to our God;

      because His judgments are true and righteous;

      for He has judged the great harlot

      who was corrupting the earth with her immorality,

      and He has avenged the blood

      of His bond-servants on her."

    (2) 2nd Stanza – *Hallelujah, the Smoke of Victory (19:3)*

      "Hallelujah! Her smoke rises up forever and ever."

---

[84] This outliner believes the *singers* in 19:1-4 are angels of various ranks. Verse 5 (the 3rd stanza) invites the *"slaves"* and *"prophets"* to join their choir.

(3) Encore – 4/24 *"Amen. Hallelujah!" (19:4)*

(4) 3rd Stanza – The Heavenly Command *(19:5; cf. 18:20)*

Everyone Join In![85]

(a) A Voice *"from the throne"* in Heaven *(19:5a)*

(b) A Voice to the Slaves in Heaven *(19:5b)*

"Give Praise to God, all you His bond-servants, you who fear Him, the small and the great."

ii. More *Angelic* Praise *(19:6-8)*

(1) The Majestic *Choir (19:6a-b)*[86]

(a) Their *Quantity* – A Countless Multitude *(19:6a)*

(b) Their *Quality* – A Thunderous Noise *(19:6b)*

(2) The Marriage *Chorus (19:6c-8)*

THE 15TH PSALM: *The Wedding March*

(a) 1st Stanza – *The Omnipotent Reigns (19:6c-7a)*

"Hallelujah!

For the Lord our God, the Almighty, reigns.

Let us rejoice and be glad

and give the glory to Him"

(b) 2nd Stanza – *The Bride Ready (19:7b-8)*[87]

"for the marriage of the Lamb has come and His bride has made herself ready. It was given to her to clothe herself in fine linen, bright and clean; for the fine linen is the righteous acts of the saints."

---

[85] In response to 18:20, all in heaven are to join. There is precedent for the ever widening circles of worshipers in scenes depicting the God's throne. Here, their exact words are not specifically stated.

[86] There are several times when a *"voice from the throne"* is hard to identify. Here it seems to be an angelic choir (cf. 14:2, where the sound of *"many waters"* and *"voice of thunder"* are angels). The angels are referring to the *"bride"* in the 3rd person.

[87] The *"marriage"* (Rev. 19:7) of the *"bride"* (the Church) takes place in heaven after the rapture (see Diagrams 5 and 6) and before she returns to earth with Christ to establish His kingdom, i.e., Christ's Millennial Reign. The *"bride"* metaphor will ultimately expand to include all the saved of all ages (cf. 21:9ff.). See Diagram 5 for a time-line of events.

b. The *Message* for John *(19:9-10)*

   i. The *Communicator* to John – An Angel *(19:9a)*

   ii. The *Command* for John – *"write"* *(19:9a)*

   iii. The *Content* to be Written – The Marriage Supper *(19:9b)*

     (1) Blessed are the *Summoned (19:9b)*

     (2) Blessed is the *Supper (19:9b)*[88]

   iv. The *Confirmation* from the Angel – *"true words"* *(19:9c)*

   v. The *Confusion* of John *(19:10)*

     (1) His *Reverence* for the Angel *(19:10a)*

     (2) The *Rebuke* of the Angel *(19:10b-c)*

       (a) Negatively – Do not worship me! *(19:10b)*

       (b) Positively – Worship God! *(19:10c)*

2. THE LORD JESUS *RETURNS (19:11-21)*

a. 1st Scene – The *Return* of Jesus Our Great King *(19:11-21)*

   i. The King's *Arrival (19:11)*[89]

     (1) His *Triumph – "white horse" (19:11a)*

     (2) His *Title – "Faithful and True" (19:11b)*

     (3) His *Truth – "in righteousness He judges" (19:11c)*

     (4) His *Terror – "wages war" (19:11d)*

   ii. The King's *Appearance (19:12-13)*

     (1) His Fiery *Eyes (19:12a)*

     (2) His Victory *Crowns (19:12b)*

     (3) His Stealthy *Name (19:12c)*

     (4) His Bloody *Robe (19:13a)*

     (5) His John 1:1 *Title* – The Word of God *(19:13b)*

   iii. The King's *Armies (19:14)*

     (1) Their White *Robes (19:14a)*

     (2) Their White *Horses (19:14b)*

---

[88] The *"marriage supper"* (9:9) seems to be a separate event from the *"marriage"* (9:7), and referring to the Millennium on earth. Those summoned (*"invited"*) are the martyred Tribulation saints (both Jew and Gentile), Tribulation saints who survive to enter the 1000-Year Kingdom, and possibly the Old Testament saints are guests as well (depending on one's view of the resurrections). See Diagram 4 for a possible resurrection scenario.

[89] Cf. Revelation 16:16 See Diagram 4 for the events associated with the Second Coming and the *War of Armageddon*.

        iv. The King's *Assault (19:15)*

             (1) His *Rout* with a Sword Tongue *(19:15a)*

             (2) His *Rule* with an Iron Rod *(19:15b)*

             (3) His *Wrath* from the Almighty *(19:15c)*

        v. The King's *Authority (19:16)*

             (1) *"KING OF KINGS" (19:16a)*

             (2) *"LORD OF LORDS" (19:16b)*

    b. 2nd Scene – The *Revenge* at the Great Supper of God *(19:17-18)*

        i. The *Birds* Called *(19:17)*

        ii. The *Bodies* Consumed *(19:18)*

    c. 3rd Scene – The *Rout* of the Great *"Beast" (19:19-21)*

        i. The *Contestants (19:19)*

             (1) The *"Beast"* and His Armies *(19:19a)*

             (2) The *"LORD"* and His Armies *(19:19b)*

        ii. The *Captured (19:20)*

             (1) The *Individuals (19:20a-b)*

                (a) The 2nd *"Beast"* – The Antichrist *(19:20a)*

                (b) The 3rd *"Beast"* – The False Prophet *(19:20b)*

             (2) Their *Incineration (19:20c)*[90]

        iii. The *Consumed* Armies *(19:21)*

             (1) *Slain* by the SWORD *(19:21a)*

             (2) *Swallowed* by the Birds *(19:21b)*

3. THE LORD JESUS *RULES (20:1-20:15)*

    a. The *Appointed* Binding of Satan *(20:1-3)*

        i. *Who?* – By an Angel *(20:1a)*

        ii. *How?* – With a Chain and Seal *(20:1b, 3b)*

        iii. *Where?* – In the Bottomless Pit *(20:1b, 3a)*

        iv. *How Long?* – For 1000 Years *(20:2, 3; cf. 4, 5, 6, 7)*[91]

        v. *Why?* – To Prevent Deception *(20:3)*

---

[90] Incinerated does not imply annihilation. They are *"tormented day and night forever."* Cf. 20:10; see Footnote 94.

[91] See an excellent treatment of the 1000 years in, *"Revelation 20 and the Millennial Debate"* by Matthew Waymeyer, (The Woodlands, Kress Christian Publications, 2004).

b. The *Anticipated* Millennial Reign of Christ *(20:4-10)*

    i. *Who? (20:4a-c)* [92]

        (1) The *Bride (20:4a, cf. 19:7-8, 14, 19)*

        (2) The *Martyrs (20:4b)*

        (3) The *Messiah (20:4c)*

    ii. *Why Them? (20:4b-d, 5, 6b)*

        (1) They *Remained* Faithful to the Messiah *(20:4b)*

        (2) They *Refrained* from *"Beast"* Worship *(20:4c)*

        (3) They *Refused* the Mark of the *"Beast" (20:4d)*

        (4) They *Rose* from the Grave *(20:5-6b)*

            (a) *Positively* – 1st Resurrection to Life *(20:5-6a)*

            (b) *Negatively* – Not 2nd Resurrection to Death *(20:6b)*

    iii. *How? (20:4a, e, 6d)*

        (1) By The *Authority* of God *(20:4a)*

        (2) In *Association* with Christ *(20:4e, 6d)*

        (3) For The *Activity* of Christ and God *(20:4a, e, 6d)*

            (a) As *Rulers* with Christ *(20:4a, e, 6d)*

            (b) As *Priests* of God and Christ *(20:6d)*

    iv. *How Long?* – 1,000 Years *(20:4e, 5, 6d, 7a; cf. 20:2-3)*

    v. The *End* of It! *(20:7b-10)*

        (1) Satan *Released (20:7b-9)*

            (a) Dragon *Freed* from Prison *(20:7b)*

            (b) Dragon *Seduced* the Nations *(20:8a-9a)*

                (i) *Generally* – 4 *"corners of the earth" (20:8a)*

                (ii) *Specifically* – *"Gog and Magog" (20:8b)*[93]

            (c) Israel *Invaded* by the Nations *(20:8c-9a)*

            (d) Jerusalem *Surrounded* by the Nations *(20:9b)*

            (e) The Nations *Consumed* by God *(20:9c)*

---

[92] The participants of Christ's Millennial Kingdom featured in this passage include the Church and those martyred in the Tribulation. We know from other texts that Gentiles saved during the Tribulation (1 Cor. 6:2), saved Israel at the end of the Tribulation (Rom. 11), and OT saints (Dan. 12:2), will also enter the 1000-Year Kingdom of Christ on earth.

[93] See Ezekiel 38:2 where *"Gog of the land of Magog"* (cf. 38:14; 39:1) describes an opponent(s) of Christ in the Tribulation. Here the opposition is at the end of the Millennium. See Diagram 4 for *"Gog and Magog"* wars.

(2) Satan *Recaptured* *(20:10)*

    (a) The Dragon *Incinerated* – By God *(20:10a)*[94]

    (b) The Devil *Incarcerated* – With Beasts *(20:10b)*

c. The *Awesome* Throne of God *(20:11)*

    i. The *Description* of It – *"great white throne"* *(20:11a)*

    ii. The *Divine* on It – *"Him who sat upon it"* *(20:11b)*

    iii. The *Disappearance* from It – *"fled away"* *(20:11c)*

d. The *Awful* Torment of the Wicked *(20:12-15)*

    i. The *People* of the Judgment *(20:12a, 13a-b)*

        (1) From the *Dead* *(20:12a, 13a-b)*

        (2) From *Small to Great* *(20:12a)*

        (3) From *Death and Hades* *(20:13b)*

    ii. The *Place* of Their Judgment – Before God *(20:12b)*

    iii. The *Purpose* of Their Judgment *(20:12b-d, 13c, 15)*

        (1) According to Their *Accounts* – *"books"* *(20:12b)*

        (2) According to the *Account* – *"the book"* *(20:12c)*

        (3) According to Their *Actions* – *"deeds"* *(20:12d, 13c)*

    iv. The *Place* of Their Punishment – *"lake of fire"* *(20:14, 15)*

4. THE LORD'S *RESIDENCE* *(21:1-22:5)*[95]

a. The *Vision* of the New Heaven and Earth *(21:1)*

b. The *General Vision* of New Jerusalem *(21:2-4)*

    i. The *Bride* from Heaven *(21:2a)*

    ii. The *Bride* for Her Husband *(21:2b)*

    iii. The *Presence* of God *(21:3)*

    iv. The *Absence* of Sorrow *(21:4; cf. 7:17b)*

c. The *Conclusion* of the *"Mystery"* *(21:5-6b)*

    i. A New *World* – *"I am making all things new."* *(21:5a)*

    ii. A True *Word* – *"these words are faithful and true."* *(21:5b)*

    iii. The *Consummation* – **IT IS DONE!** *(21:6a)*

    iv. The *Confirmation* – *"the Alpha and the Omega, the beginning and the end!"* *(21:6b)*

---

[94] Incinerated does not imply annihilation. Notice that the unholy trinity (Satan, the Beast, and the False Prophet) are *"tormented day and night forever."*

[95] See Diagrams 7 and 8 for a comparison of the *Millennial* and *New* Jerusalem.

    d. The *Invitation* to Enter New Jerusalem *(21:6c-8)*

        i. The *Prize* for Overcomers *(21:6c, 7)*

            (1) A *Satisfied* Thirst – *"spring of water of life" (21:6c)*

            (2) A *Certified* Inheritance – *"these things" (21:7a)*

            (3) A *Verified* Relationship – *"he will be My son" (21:7b)*

        ii. The *Punishment* for Unbelievers *(21:8)*

            (1) The *List* of Sinners – *"cowardly," "unbelieving,"*
"abominable," etc. *(21:8a)*

            (2) The *Lake* of Fire – *"fire and brimstone" (21:8b)*

            (3) The *Last* Death – 2nd *"death" (21:8c)*

    e. The *Specific Vision* of New Jerusalem *(21:9-22:5)*

        i. The *Delivered* Vision of Jerusalem *(21:9-10)*

            (1) The *Messenger* – *"one of the seven angels" (21:9a)*

            (2) The *Recipient* – John *(21:10)*

               (a) *In* the spirit *(21:10a)*[96]

               (b) *On* a High Mountain *(21:10b)*

            (3) The *Content* – *"the holy city, Jerusalem" (21:10b)*

        ii. The *Detailed* Vision of Jerusalem *(21:9b, 10b, 11-22:5)*[97]

            (1) Her *Name* – *"The bride, the wife of the Lamb" (21:9b)*

            (2) Her *Nature (21:10b; 21:27a; 22:3a)*

               (a) *Consecrated* – *"holy" (21:10b)*

               (b) *Corruption* Removed – No Unclean *(21:27a)*

               (c) *Curse* Removed – No Curse *(22:3a)*

            (3) Her *Glory (21:11a-b, 18b, 23b)*

               (a) *Brilliance* of God *(21:11a, 23b)*

               (b) *Brightness* of Jasper *(21:11b, 18a)*

            (4) Her *Origin* – *"of heaven from God" (21:10c)*

---

[96] Cf. Rev. 1:10; 4:2 and 17:3. See Footnote 7.

[97] More than one Scripture reference describing the features of *"new Jerusalem"* may be listed beside a point in the outline. Some descriptions from Rev. 21:9-22:5 are repeated in more than one verse. These details have been grouped for outlining purposes. See Footnote 1.

(5) Her *Wall (21:12a, 15-17, 18a)*

    (a) Its *Magnitude* – "great and high" *(21:12a)*

    (b) Its *Measurer* – The Angel *(21:15)*

    (c) Its *Material* – "jasper" *(21:18a)*

    (d) Its *Measurements (21:16-17)*

        (i) The City's *Height* – 1,500 Miles *(21:16)*

        (ii) The City's *Length* – 1,500 Miles *(21:16)*

        (iii) The Wall's *Width* – 72 Yards Thick *(21:17)*

(6) Her *Foundation Stones (21:14, 19-20)*

    (a) The *Names* on Them – 12 Apostles *(21:14)*

    (b) The *Nature* of Them – 12 Stones *(21:19-20)*

(7) Her *Gates (21:12b-d, 13, 21a-b)*

    (a) Their *Aggregate* – 12 *(21:12b, 21a)*

    (b) Their *Attendants (21:12c)*

        (i) Their *Name* – "angels" *(21:12c)*

        (ii) Their *Number* – 12 *(21:12c)*

    (c) Their *Arrangement* – 3 On Each Side *(21:13)*

    (d) Their *Association* – 1 For Each Tribe *(21:12d)*

    (e) Their *Appearance* – Each A Single Pearl *(21:21b)*

(8) Her *Street* – "like transparent glass" *(21:21c)*

(9) Her *Temple (21:22)*

    (a) No Need of A Temple *(21:22a)*

    (b) The Lord and the Lamb *(21:22b)*

(10) Her *River (22:1)*

    (a) Its *Substance* – the "water of life" *(22:1a)*

    (b) Its *Source* – "throne of God" *(22:1b)*

(11) Her *Tree (22:2)*

    (a) *Covering* Each Side of the River *(22:2a)*

    (b) *Bearing* 12 Kinds of Fruit Each Month *(22:2b)*

    (c) *Healing* the Nations *(22:2c)*

(12) Her *Inhabitants (21:24, 26, 27b; 22:3c; 24a-b, 5c)*

    (a) *Serve* the Lamb *(22:3c)*

    (b) *See* the Lamb *(22:4a)*

    (c) *Wear* the Name of the Lamb *(22:4b)*

    (d) *Written* in the *"Lamb's book of life" (21:27b)*

    (e) *Reign* with the Lamb *(22:5c)*

    (f) *Reside* in New Earth – *"nations" (21:24, 26)*[98]

(13) Her *Throne* – *"of God and of the Lamb" (22:3b)*

(14) Her *Lights (21:23; 22:5a-b)*[99]

    (a) No *Night (21:25b; 22:5)*

    (b) No Need of *Luminaries (21:23a; 22:5ab)*

    (c) The Lord *Illumines (21:23b; 22:5c)*

    (d) The Lamb *Illumines (21:23c; 22:5c)*

---

[98] The *"nations"* are mentioned 3 times as residents of the *"new heaven," "new earth"* and *"new Jerusalem."* This is a clear reference to the redeemed from *"every tribe, tongue and nation"* dwelling together in unity (possibly maintaining their nationalities).

[99] See Genesis 1:3.

PART 4

THE INVITATIONS! *(22:6-21)*

I.   **The Angel's <u>Witness</u>** *(22:6)*

   A.   A *Sure* Revelation *(22:6a)*

      1.   *Faithful* Words *(22:6a)*

      2.   *Factual* Words *(22:6a)*

   B.   A *Sent* Revelation *(22:6b-d)*

      1.   Words *from* God Himself *(22:6b)*

      2.   Words *for* God's Servants *(22:6c)*

      3.   Words *in* God's Timing *(22:6d)*

II.   **Jesus' 1st <u>Invitation</u>** *(22:7)*

   A.   From the One Who Comes *Speedily (22:7a; cf. 12a, 20)*

   B.   From the One Who Blesses *Surely (22:7b)*

III.   **John's <u>Testimony</u>** *(22:8-11)*

   A.   The Angel's Incredible *Revelation (22:8a)*

   B.   John's Incorrect *Response (22:8b-c)*

      1.   *Hearing* the Angel *(22:8b)*

      2.   *Falling* Before the Angel *(22:8b)*[100]

      3.   *Worshiping* the Angel *(22:8c)*

   C.   The Angel's Invoking *Rebuke (22:9-11)*

      1.   *Worship* God! – *"Worship God." (22:9)*

      2.   *Wrap* It Up! – *"Do not seal up" (22:10a)*[101]

      3.   *Wake* Up! – *"the time is near" (22:10b)*

---

[100] This is the second time that John has an improper response to the angel's words (Rev. 19:10).
[101] Daniel was to seal up his prophecy, since more was forthcoming (Dan. 12:9). Here, the prophecy is not sealed, since it is complete and now ready for reading and heeding.

4. *Warning* for the Wicked *(22:11)*

   a. The Condition and Continuation of the Wicked –
   "the one who does wrong, still do wrong" (22:11a)

   b. The Condition and Continuation of the Righteous –
   "the one who is righteous, still practice
   righteousness" (22:11b)

IV. **Jesus' 2nd Invitation** *(22:12-16)*

A. **Come to the *Rewarder*!** – *"My reward is with me" (22:12)*

B. **Come to the *LORD*!** *(22:13)*

   1. The *"Alpha and Omega" (22:13a)*

   2. The *"Beginning and the End" (22:13b)*

   3. The *"First and the Last" (22:13c)*

C. **Hope in the *Redeemer*!** *(22:14)*

   1. Blessing from the *Conveyor* of Salvation *(22:14a)*

   2. Blessing from the *Creator* of Life *(22:14a)*

   3. Blessing from the *Constructer* of The City *(22:14a)*

D. **Heed the *Gatekeeper*!** – *"outside are dogs," etc. (22:15)*

E. **Hear His *Messenger*!** – *"I have sent My angel" (22:16a)*

F. **Hurry To the *Messiah*!** *(22:16b-c)*

   1. The *"root and descendant of David" (22:16b)*

   2. The *"bright morning star" (22:16c)*

V. **The 3rd Invitation** *(22:17)*

A. **From the *Spirit*** – *"come" (22:17a)*

B. **From the *Bride*** – *"come" (22:17a)*

C. **From *Jesus (22:17b-d)***

   1. To All Who Hear – *"come" (22:17b)*

   2. To All Who Thirst – *"come" (22:17c)*

   3. To All The Poor – *"come" (22:17d)*

VI.   Jesus' <u>Caution</u> (22:18-19)[102]

    A.   Don't *Discount* It! – *"I testify to every one . . ." (22:18a)*

    B.   Don't *Add*! – *"if anyone adds . . ." (22:18b)*

    C.   Don't *Subtract*! – *"if anyone takes away . . ." (22:19a)*

    D.   Don't Be *Added To*! – *"God will add to him . . ." (22:18c)*

    E.   Don't Be *Subtracted From*! – *"God will take away . . ."*
    (22:19b)

VII. Jesus' 4th and Final <u>Invitation</u> (22:20)

    A.   Jesus' *Announcement*: *"I am coming quickly."*
    (22:20a; cf. 7a, 12a)

    B.   John's *Appeal*: *"Amen, even so, come, Lord Jesus!" (22:20b)*

VIII. John's <u>Benediction</u> (22:21)

    "May the grace of our Lord Jesus Christ be with you all.[103] Amen."

---

[102] See Deut. 4:2, *"You shall not add to the word which I am commanding you, nor take away from it, . . ."* The messengers (stars, Rev. 1:20), in the spirit of Moses, were to guard the contents of this prophecy. This being the last prophetic word given by Christ, through his apostles, agues heavily for the application applied to the rest of Scripture. There is no need for any further revelation since, *"His divine power has granted to us everything pertaining to life and godliness . . ."* (2 Pet. 1:3).

[103] Because you're going to need it!

^{2:1} "To the angel of the church in **Ephesus** write:

The One who holds the seven stars in His right hand, the One who walks among the seven golden lampstands, says this:

² '**I know** your deeds and your toil and perseverance, and that you cannot tolerate evil men, and you put to the test those who call themselves apostles, and they are not, and you found them *to be* false; ³ and you have perseverance and have endured for My name's sake, and have not grown weary.

⁴ '**But I have *this* against you,** that you have left your first love.

⁵ '**Remember therefore from where you have fallen, and repent and do the deeds you did at first; or else I am coming to you, and will remove your lampstand out of its place-- unless you repent.** ⁶ '**Yet this you do have, that you hate the deeds of the Nicolaitans, which I also hate.**

⁷ '**He who has an ear, let him hear what the Spirit says to the churches. To him who overcomes,** I will give to eat of the tree of life, which is in the Paradise of God.'

---

⁸ "And to the angel of the church in **Smyrna** write:

The first and the last, who was dead, and has come to life, says this:

⁹ '**I know** your tribulation and your poverty (but you are rich), and the blasphemy by those who say they are Jews and are not, but are a synagogue of Satan.

¹⁰ '**Do not fear** what you are about to suffer. Behold, the devil is about to cast some of you into prison, that you may be tested, and you will have tribulation ten days. **Be faithful** until death, and I will give you the crown of life.

¹¹ '**He who has an ear, let him hear what the Spirit says to the churches. He who overcomes** shall not be hurt by the second death.'

---

¹² "And to the angel of the church in **Pergamum** write:

The One who has the sharp two-edged sword says this:

¹³ '**I know** where you dwell, <u>where Satan's throne is</u>; and you hold fast My name, and did not deny My faith, even in the days of Antipas, My witness, My faithful one, who was killed among you, <u>where Satan dwells</u>.

¹⁴ '**But I have a few things against you,** because you have there some who hold the teaching of Balaam, who kept teaching Balak to put a stumbling block before the sons of Israel, to eat things sacrificed to idols, and to commit *acts of* immorality. ¹⁵ So you also have some who in the same way hold the teaching of the <u>Nicolaitans</u>.

¹⁶ '**Repent therefore; or else I am coming to you quickly, and I will make war against them with the sword of My mouth.**

¹⁷ '**He who has an ear, let him hear** what the Spirit says to the churches. To **him who overcomes,** to him I will give *some* of the hidden manna, and I will give him a white stone, and a new name written on the stone which no one knows but he who receives it.'

---

¹⁸ "And to the angel of the church in **Thyatira** write:

The Son of God, who has eyes like a flame of fire, and His feet are like burnished bronze, says this:

¹⁹ '**I know** your deeds, and your love and faith and service and perseverance, and that your deeds of late are greater than at first.

²⁰ '**But I have *this* against you,** that you tolerate the woman Jezebel, who calls herself a prophetess, and she teaches and leads My bond-servants astray, so that they commit *acts of* immorality and eat things sacrificed to idols. ²¹ 'And I gave her time to repent; and she does not want to repent of her immorality. ²² 'Behold, I will cast her upon a bed *of sickness*, and those who commit adultery with her into great tribulation, unless they repent of her deeds. ²³ 'And I will kill her children with pestilence; and all the churches will know that I am He who searches the minds and hearts; and I will give to each one of you according to your deeds. ²⁴ 'But I say to you, the rest who are in Thyatira, who do not hold this teaching, who have not known the deep things of Satan, as they call them-- I place no other burden on you.

²⁵ '**Nevertheless what you have, hold fast until I come.**

²⁶ 'And **he who overcomes**, and he who keeps My deeds until the end, to him I will give authority over the nations; ²⁷ and he shall rule them with a rod of iron, as the vessels of the potter are broken to pieces, as I also have received *authority* from My Father; ²⁸ and I will give him the morning star. ²⁹ '**He who has an ear, let him hear what the Spirit says to the churches.'**

3:1 "To the angel of the church in **Sardis** write:

He who has the seven Spirits of God, and the seven stars, says this:

'**I know** your deeds, that you have a name that you are alive, but you are dead.

2 '**Wake up, and strengthen the things that remain, which were about to die; for I have not found your deeds completed in the sight of My God.** 3 **So 'Remember what you have received and heard; and keep** *it,* **and repent. Therefore if you do not wake up, I will come like a thief, and you will not know at what hour I will come to you.**

4 'But you have a few people in Sardis who have not soiled their garments; and they will walk with Me in white; for they are worthy.

5 '**He who overcomes** will thus be clothed in white garments; and I will not erase his name from the book of life, and I will confess his name before My Father, and before His angels. 6 '**He who has an ear, let him hear what the Spirit says to the churches.'**

---

7 "And to the angel of the church in **Philadelphia** write:

He who is holy, who is true, who has the key of David, who opens and no one will shut, and who shuts and no one opens, says this:

8 '**I know** your deeds. Behold, I have put before you an open door which no one can shut, because you have a little power, and have kept My word, and have not denied My name.

9 'Behold, I will cause *those* of the synagogue of Satan, who say that they are Jews, and are not, but lie--I will make them come and bow down at your feet, and make them know that I have loved you.

10 'Because you have kept the word of My perseverance, I also will keep you from the hour of testing, that *hour* which is about to come upon the whole world, to test those who dwell on the earth.

11 'I am coming quickly; **hold fast what you have, so that no one will take your crown.**

12 '**He who overcomes**, I will make him a pillar in the temple of My God, and he will not go out from it anymore; and I will write on him the name of My God, and the name of the city of My God, the new Jerusalem, which comes down out of heaven from My God, and My new name. 13 '**He who has an ear, let him hear what the Spirit says to the churches.'**

---

14 "To the angel of the church in **Laodicea** write:

The Amen, the faithful and true Witness, the Beginning of the creation of God, says this:

15 '**I know** your deeds, that you are neither cold nor hot; I wish that you were cold or hot. 16 So because you are lukewarm, and neither hot nor cold, I will spit you out of My mouth. 17 'Because you say, "I am rich, and have become wealthy, and have need of nothing," and you do not know that you are wretched and miserable and poor and blind and naked,

18 **I advise you to buy from Me gold refined by fire,** so that you may become rich, and white garments, that you may clothe yourself, and *that* the shame of your nakedness will not be revealed; and eye salve to anoint your eyes, so that you may see.

19 'Those whom I love, I reprove and discipline; therefore **be zealous, and repent**. 20 'Behold, I stand at the door and knock; if anyone hears My voice and opens the door, I will come in to him and will dine with him, and he with Me.

21 '**He who overcomes**, I will grant to him to sit down with Me on My throne, as I also overcame and sat down with My Father on His throne. 22 '**He who has an ear, let him hear what the Spirit says to the churches.**

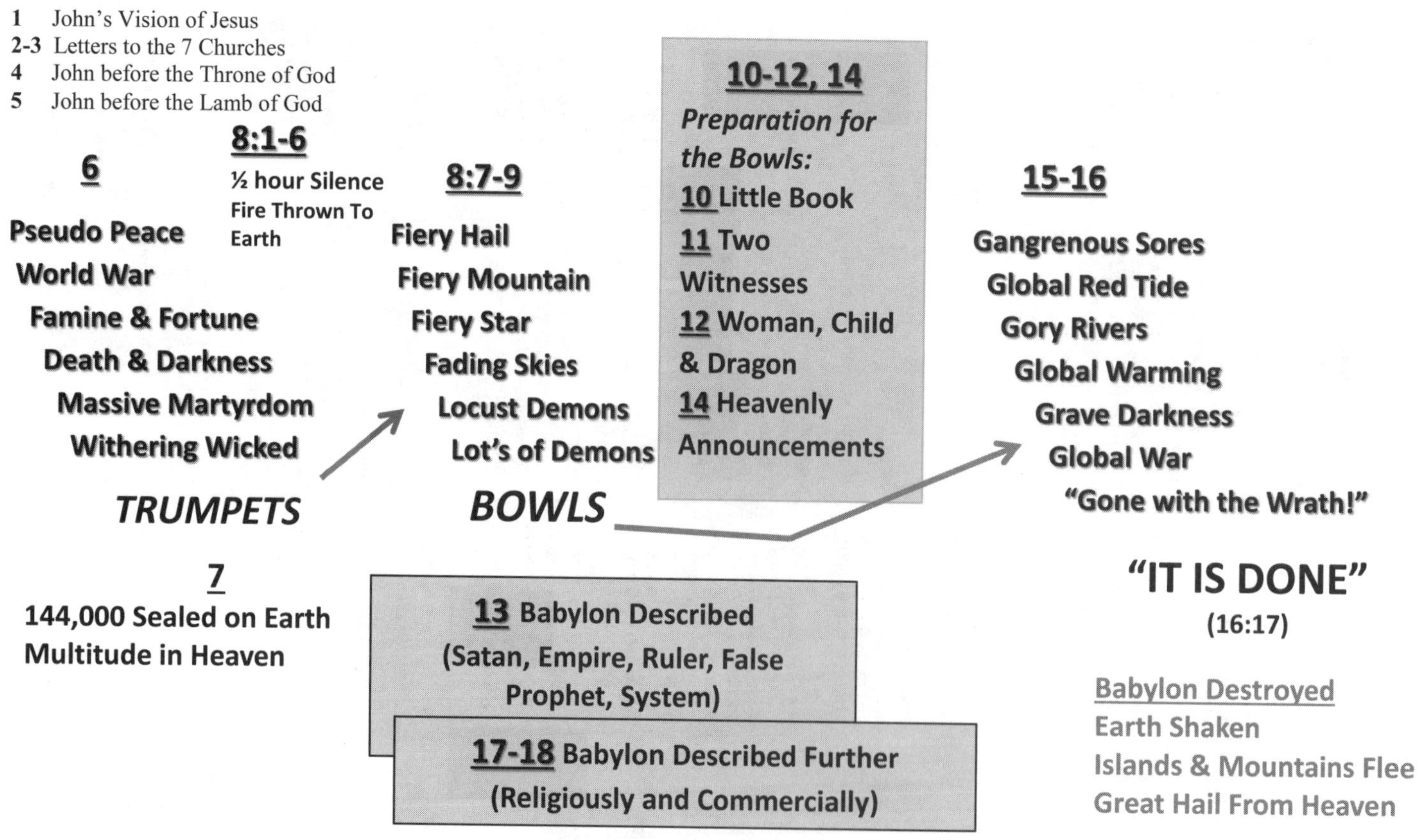

1 John's Vision of Jesus
2-3 Letters to the 7 Churches
4 John before the Throne of God
5 John before the Lamb of God

6

Pseudo Peace
World War
Famine & Fortune
Death & Darkness
Massive Martyrdom
Withering Wicked

8:1-6

½ hour Silence
Fire Thrown To Earth

TRUMPETS

7

144,000 Sealed on Earth
Multitude in Heaven

8:7-9

Fiery Hail
Fiery Mountain
Fiery Star
Fading Skies
Locust Demons
Lot's of Demons

BOWLS

10-12, 14

Preparation for the Bowls:
10 Little Book
11 Two Witnesses
12 Woman, Child & Dragon
14 Heavenly Announcements

13 Babylon Described
(Satan, Empire, Ruler, False Prophet, System)

17-18 Babylon Described Further
(Religiously and Commercially)

15-16

Gangrenous Sores
Global Red Tide
Gory Rivers
Global Warming
Grave Darkness
Global War
"Gone with the Wrath!"

"IT IS DONE"
(16:17)

Babylon Destroyed
Earth Shaken
Islands & Mountains Flee
Great Hail From Heaven

Diagram 2 "Ordering Revelation's Chapters"

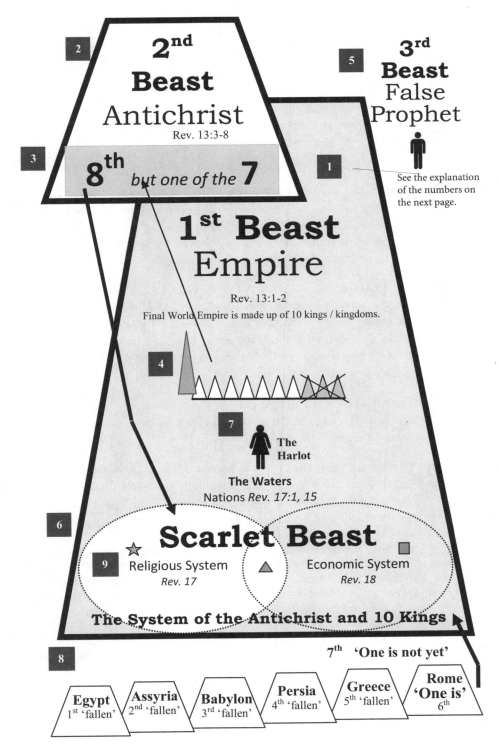

2   **2nd Beast** Antichrist Rev. 13:3-8

5   **3rd Beast** False Prophet

3

8th *but one of the* **7**

1   See the explanation of the numbers on the next page.

1st Beast Empire

Rev. 13:1-2

Final World Empire is made up of 10 kings / kingdoms.

4

7   The Harlot

The Waters
Nations *Rev. 17:1, 15*

6

Scarlet Beast

9   ☆ Religious System *Rev. 17*   △   ▢ Economic System *Rev. 18*

The System of the Antichrist and 10 Kings

8

7th 'One is not yet'

| Egypt 1st 'fallen' | Assyria 2nd 'fallen' | Babylon 3rd 'fallen' | Persia 4th 'fallen' | Greece 5th 'fallen' | Rome 'One is' 6th |

1 The **1ˢᵗ beast** is the last days' dominant world Empire made up of 10 *"horns"* (kings / kingdoms). He will set up a military post 'between Jerusalem and the Mediterranean' (Dan. 11:45), maybe a Fort Bragg-like location. See Dan. 2:41-43; 7:23-24; cf. Rev. 17:8- 18.

2 The **2ⁿᵈ Beast** (the Antichrist) is the leader of the last days' dominant Empire (Dan. 7:24b-26; 11:26-45; Matt.24:15; 2 Thess. 2:4-5; Rev. 13:3-8).

3 The **8ᵗʰ but one of the 7** refers to Rev. 17:11, where the *"scarlet beast"* is an *"eighth and is one of the seven."* After the Antichrist's *"fatal wound is healed"* and he comes *"out of the abyss,"* he will become so powerful that he will be his own kingdom, even though he is part of, and over, the 7ᵗʰ kingdom (*"mountain" / "head"*).

4 The **10 Horns** (Rev 13:1; 17:3,11) represent 10 kings / kingdoms that rule the last days' world Empire and *"give their power and authority to the beast,"* i.e. the Antichrist (Dan. 2:41-42; 7:16-24; Rev. 17:12-13). Daniel 7:20 states that the *"little horn"* (the 11ᵗʰ *"horn"* – Antichrist), grows to be a large powerful *"horn,"* and will remove 3 of the 10 kings at some point (Dan. 7:8).

5 The **3ʳᵈ Beast** (the False Prophet) is the promoter of the 2ⁿᵈ *"Beast"* during the Tribulation. He causes all to get the mark of the Beast and worship him.

6 The **Scarlet Beast** (Rev 17:3) is another designation for the last days' Empire (Rev. 13:1-2; 17:8-11), particularly its leader (the 2ⁿᵈ Beast) who *"was and is not, and is about to come up out of the abyss."* The Empire and its leader are synonymous.

7 The **Harlot (*'Mystery Babylon'*)** sits on the backs of "many waters" (the previous world empires), including the back of the last days' Empire (the 7ᵗʰ *"head"* or 7ᵗʰ *"mountain"*) and its leader - the *'Scarlet Beast'*. The 'Woman' is a religious and secular seducer that draws earth-dwellers into the grips of the 10 Kings and the Antichrist.

God will cause the 2ⁿᵈ *'Beast'* (Antichrist) and the 10 to destroy the *'Harlot'* (the anti-God seducing influence) presumably after using her to secure power. The False Prophet will then cause all to worship the 2ⁿᵈ *'Beast'* instead of following the enticing *'Harlot'*.

8 Rev. 17:9-10, *"The seven heads are seven mountains on which the woman sits, and they are seven kings' five have fallen, one is, the other has not yet come; and when he comes, he must remain a little while."*

9 *'BABYLON'* the *'Harlot'* (the seducing influence), who *'sits on many waters'* (nations) and is used by the Antichrist, seems to have a capital city (or cities) in Revelation 17 and 18. Some believe that both capitals may occupy the same location, possibly on the ruins of ancient Babylon.

⭐ **The religious system capital,** <u>maybe</u> a *Rome-like* city. It will be destroyed by the Antichrist and the 10 kings (Rev. 17:16), probably at the time the Antichrist moves into the temple to declare himself to be God (Dan. 7:26; Matt. 24:15; Thess. 2:3-5), making Jerusalem his own religious capital.

◻ **The political / economic capital** will be destroyed at Christ's coming (Rev. 18:9), <u>maybe</u> a *Dubai-like* city.

▲ **The Military Post**

Diagram 4 "Event Chart"

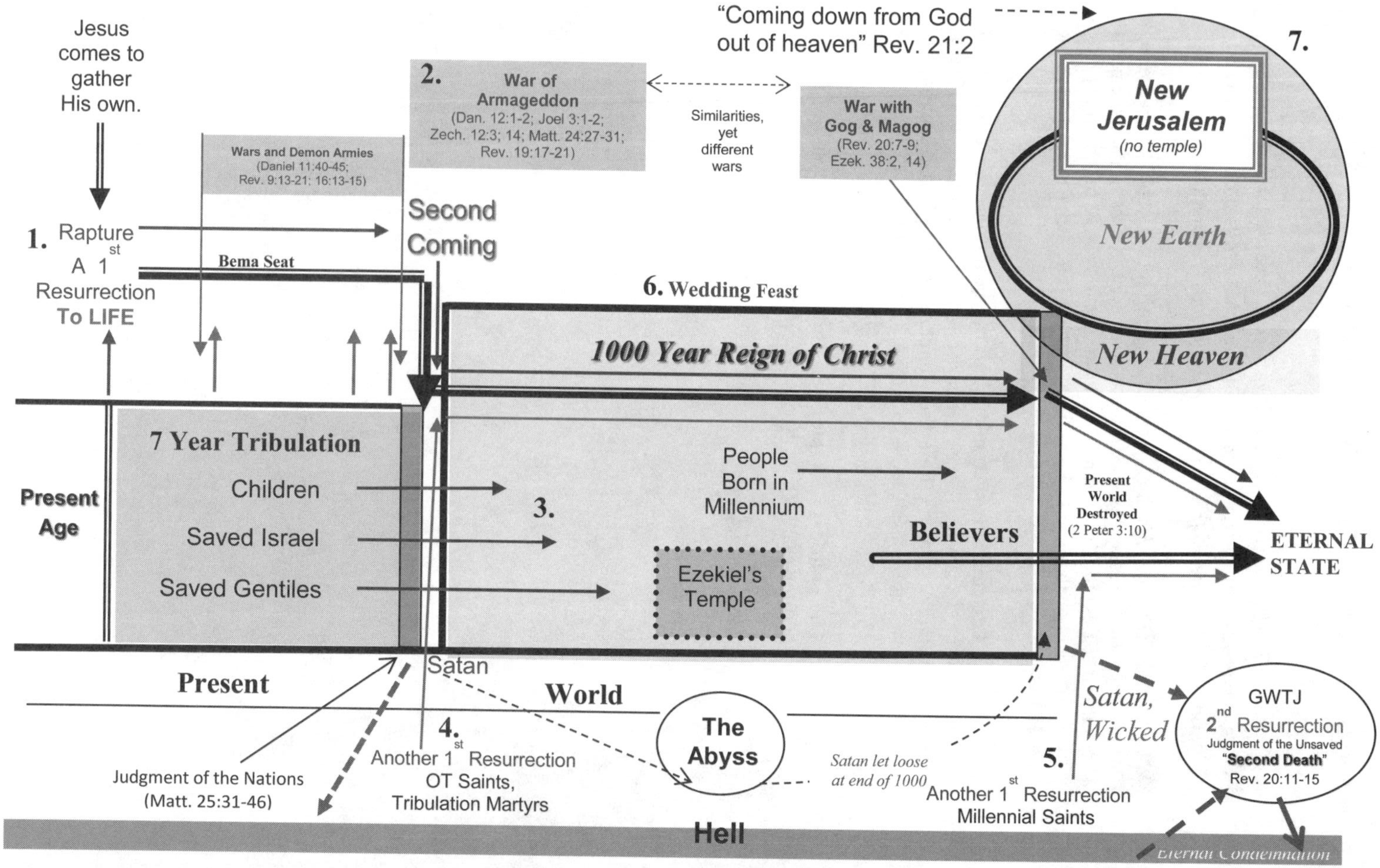

Jesus comes to gather His own.

1. Rapture
A 1st Resurrection
To LIFE

Present Age

Bema Seat

Wars and Demon Armies
(Daniel 11:40-45;
Rev. 9:13-21; 16:13-15)

7 Year Tribulation
Children
Saved Israel
Saved Gentiles

Present

Judgment of the Nations
(Matt. 25:31-46)

2. War of Armageddon
(Dan. 12:1-2; Joel 3:1-2;
Zech. 12:3, 14; Matt. 24:27-31;
Rev. 19:17-21)

Second Coming

3.
1000 Year Reign of Christ

6. Wedding Feast

People Born in Millennium

Ezekiel's Temple

World

Satan

4. Another 1st Resurrection
OT Saints,
Tribulation Martyrs

The Abyss

Satan let loose at end of 1000

Hell

5. Another 1st Resurrection
Millennial Saints

Believers

Present World Destroyed (2 Peter 3:10)

War with Gog & Magog
(Rev. 20:7-9;
Ezek. 38:2, 14)

Similarities, yet different wars

"Coming down from God out of heaven" Rev. 21:2

7.

New Jerusalem
(no temple)

New Earth

New Heaven

ETERNAL STATE

Satan, Wicked

GWTJ
2nd Resurrection
Judgment of the Unsaved
"Second Death"
Rev. 20:11-15

Eternal Condemnation

1. There are four Rapture Views: *Pre-tribulation; Mid-tribulation; Pre-wrath; Post-tribulation.* See Diagram 5 for a defense of the Pre-tribulation view.

2. Battles begin on the mountains of Israel (Ezek. 38-39) and on "Har (Mt.) of Magedon," i.e. *War of Armageddon.* The campaign ends up in Jerusalem in a confrontation with Jesus (Zech. 12-14). Though there are similar descriptions and names ("Gog") used in Ezekiel and Revelation, there are two distinct major battles – one at the end of the Tribulation and one at the end of the Millennium.

3. The *"all Israel* (that) *will be saved"* at the end of the Tribulation will enter into the Kingdom (Romans 9:26) along with Gentiles who will be saved during that time. It <u>may</u> be that children will inherit the Kingdom as well (Matthew 19:13).

4. The resurrection of Old Testament and Tribulation saints seem to occur at the end of the Tribulation (Dan. 12). They will enter Christ's Millennial Kingdom. Admittedly, the interaction of the glorified Church, resurrected Old Testament and Tribulation saints, and those who enter the Kingdom in their physical bodies, is unspecified in Scripture.

5. If it is the case that those who become believers during the Millennial Kingdom may still die (albeit at an old age; Isaiah 65:20), they would be raised and glorified at the end of that period. The *"first resurrection"* is one of *kind* not *time.* The Rapture and the resurrection of OT saints and Tribulation saints, although separated, constitute a resurrection *"to life."* The *"second death"* will be the resurrection and judgment of unbelievers of all time.

6. The *"marriage of the Lamb"* and the *"marriage supper of the Lamb"* are two separate events. The raptured saints are dressed in white and return with the Lord at the end of the Tribulation. The celebration of that marriage lasts throughout the Millennium. Following the 1,000-Year reign of Christ, the *"bride of Christ"* metaphor will expand to include all saints of all time.

6. Although there are no descriptions of *"a new heaven and a new earth,"* there are descriptions and dimensions of the "New Jerusalem" are given in Revelation 21:1 through 22:4.

The nature of events at Christ's posttribulational coming (Matt. 24:31)
radically differs from that of the rapture (1 Thess 4:16-17).

RAPTURE	SECOND COMING
1. Christ gathers His own *(1 Thess. 4:16–17)*	Angels gather the elect *(Matt.24:31)*
2. Resurrection is prominent *(4:15–16)*	No mention of resurrection
3. Christ comes to reward *(1 Cor. 3:11-1; 2 Cor. 5:10)*	Christ comes to judge *(Matt.25:31–46)*
4. Believers depart the earth *(1 Thess. 4:15–17)*	Unbelievers are taken away *(Matt. 24:37–41)*
Unbelievers remain on the earth *(implied)*	Believers remain on the earth *(Matt. 25:34)*
5. No talk of setting up set the kingdom	Clear talk of Christ coming to up a kingdom *(Matt. 25:31, 34)*
6. Believers receive glorified bodies *(1 Cor. 15:51–57)*	No one receives glorified bodies
7. Christ comes in the air *(1 Thess. 4:17)*	Christ comes on the earth *(Matt. 25:31–32)*

*Additionally, parables in Matthew 13 confirm differences between
the rapture and the final event of Christ's second coming.*

8. Believers are removed from from among unbelievers *(1 Thess. 4:15-17)*	Tares (unbeliever) taken out among the wheat (believers) *(Matt. 13:30, 40)*
9. Believers are removed from taken out among unbelievers (believers) *(1 Thess. 4:17)*	The bad fish (unbelievers) from among the good fish *(Matt. 25:31–32)*

Taken from Dr. Richard Mayhue, "Why A Pretribulation Rapture?" in *Christ's Prophetic Plans*, John MacArthur and Richard Mayhue (Chicago, Moody Publishers, 2012), 93-94.

MILLENNIAL JERUSALEM	ETERNAL JERUSALEM
### *CITY* ***Ezekiel 42:15-20*** He measured it on the four sides; it had a wall all around, the length five hundred and the width five hundred, to divide between the holy and the profane. (1 X 1 mile, temple area) ***Ezekiel 48:15-17*** 1.65 X 1.65 miles for the city.	### *CITY* ***Rev 21:16*** The city is laid out as a square, and its length is as great as the width; and he measured the city with the rod, fifteen hundred miles; its length and width and height are equal.
### *WALLS* ***Isaiah 60:10*** "Foreigners will build up your walls, and their kings will minister to you; for in My wrath I struck you, and in My favor I have had compassion on you. ***Ezekiel 40:5*** 875 ft. X 10 ½ ft. high and 10 ½ ft. wide on each side (temple complex)	### *WALLS* ***Rev 21:17-20*** And he measured its wall, seventy-two yards, *according to* human measurements, which are *also* angelic *measurements*. The material of the wall was jasper; and the city was pure gold, like clear glass. The foundation stones of the city wall were adorned with every kind of precious stone.
### *GATES* ***Isaiah 60:11-12*** "Your gates will be open continually; they will not be closed day or night, so that *men* may bring to you the wealth of the nations, with their kings led in procession. For the nation and the kingdom which will not serve you will perish, and the nations will be utterly ruined." ***Ezekiel 48:30-34*** Gates have names of 12 tribes.	### *GATES* ***Rev 21:21*** "And the twelve gates were twelve pearls; each one of the gates was a single pearl. And the street of the city was pure gold, like transparent glass." ***Rev 21:25-26*** "In the daytime (for there will be no night there) its gates will never be closed; and they will bring the glory and the honor of the nations into it; . . ." ***Rev 21:12-14*** Gates have names of 12 tribes & apostles.
### *TEMPLE* ***Ezekiel 40:5-42:20*** (descriptions of the temple)	### *TEMPLE* ***Rev 21:22*** "I saw no temple in it, for the Lord God the Almighty and the Lamb are its temple."
### *DEATH* ***Isaiah 65:20*** "No longer will there be in it an infant *who lives but a few* days, or an old man who does not live out his days; for the youth will die at the age of one hundred and the one who does not reach the age of one hundred will be *thought* accursed."	### *DEATH* ***Rev 21:4*** ". . . and He will wipe away every tear from their eyes; and there will be no longer be *any* death; there will no longer be *any* mourning, or crying, or pain; the first things have passed

MILLENNIAL JERUSALEM	ETERNAL JERUSALEM
### RIVER ***Ezekiel 47:1*** "Then he brought me back to the door of the house; and behold, water was flowing <u>from under the threshold of the house</u> toward the east, for the house faced east." ***Zechariah 14:8*** "In that day living waters will flow out of Jerusalem, half of them toward the eastern sea and the other half toward the western sea."	### RIVER ***Rev 22:1-2*** "Then he showed me a river of the water of life, clear as crystal, <u>coming from the throne of God</u> and of the Lamb, [2] in the middle of the street. . ."
### TREES ***Ezekiel 47:7*** "Now when I had returned, behold, <u>on the bank</u> of the river there *were* very many <u>trees</u> on the one side and on the other."	### TREE ***Rev 22:2*** in the middle of its street. On either side of the river was <u>the tree of life</u>, bearing twelve *kinds of* fruit, yielding its fruit every month; and the leaves of the tree were for the healing of the nations.
### LIGHTS ***Isaiah 30:26*** "The light of the moon will be as the light of the sun, and the light of the sun will be seven times *brighter,* like the light of seven days, on the day the LORD binds up the fracture of His people and heals the bruise He has inflicted."	### LIGHTS ***Isaiah 60:19-20*** "No longer will you have the sun for light by day, Nor for brightness will the moon give you light; but you will have the LORD for an everlasting light, and your God for your glory. [20] "Your sun will no longer set, nor will your moon wane; for you will have the LORD for an everlasting light, and the days of your mourning will be over. ***Revelation 21:22*** "I saw no temple in it, for the Lord God the Almighty and the Lamb are its temple. [23] And the city has no need of the sun or of the moon to shine on it, for the glory of God has illumined it, and its lamp *is* the Lamb."
### SEA ***Ezekiel 45 & 48; Zech. 14:8*** lists the Mediterranean and Dead Seas as boundaries.	### SEA ***Rev 21:1*** "Then I saw a new heaven and a new earth; for the first heaven and the first earth passed away, and there is no longer *any* sea."

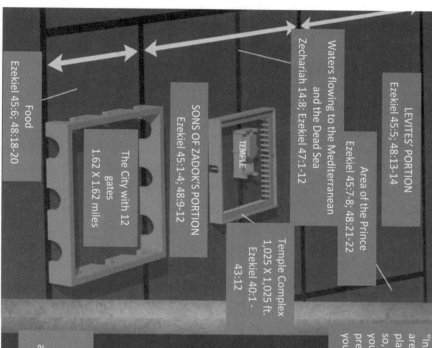

LEVITES' PORTION
Ezekiel 45:5; 48:13-14

Waters flowing to the Mediterranean
and the Dead Sea
Zechariah 14:8; Ezekiel 47:1-12

Area of the Prince
Ezekiel 45:7-8; 48:21-22

SONS OF ZADOK'S PORTION
Ezekiel 45:1-4; 48:9-12

TEMPLE

The City with 12
gates
1.62 X 1.62 miles

Temple Complex
1,025 X 1,025 ft.
Ezekiel 40:1 -
43:12

Food
Ezekiel 45:6; 48:18-20

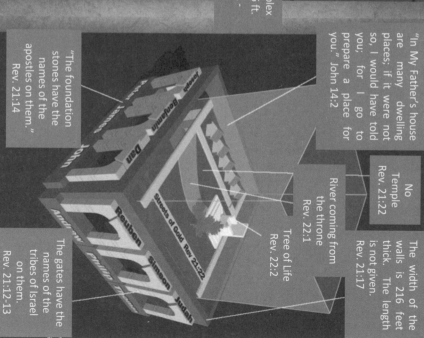

"In My Father's house
are many dwelling
places; if it were not
so, I would have told
you; for I go to
prepare a place for
you." John 14:2

"The foundation
stones have the
names of the
apostles on them."
Rev. 21:14

No
Temple
Rev. 21:22

The width of the
walls is 216 feet
thick. The length
is not given.
Rev. 21:17

River coming from
the throne
Rev. 22:1

Tree of Life
Rev. 22:2

The gates have the
names of the
tribes of Israel
on them.
Rev. 21:12-13